ACADEMIA LUNARE
Call For Papers 2022

Follow Me.
Religion in Fantasy and Science Fiction

Edited By
Francesca T Barbini

Introduction © Francesca T Barbini 2023
Articles © is with each individual author 2023
Cover Design © Francesca T Barbini 2023
Cover Image: The Singer of Amun Nany's Funerary Papyrus - Book of the Dead

First published by Luna Press Publishing, Edinburgh, 2023

Follow Me. Religion in Fantasy and Science Fiction © 2021. All rights reserved. No part of this publication may be reproduced, stored in a retrieval system, or transmitted in any form or by any means, electronic, mechanical, photocopy, recording or otherwise, without prior written permission of the copyright owners. Nor can it be circulated in any form of binding or cover other than that in which it is published and without similar condition including this condition being imposed on a subsequent purchaser.

www.lunapresspublishing.com

ISBN-13: 978-1-915556-18-9

Academia Lunare CfPs Series

Gender Identity and Sexuality in Fantasy and Science Fiction (2017)
Winner of the British Fantasy Society Awards
1 Article Shortlisted for the BSFA Awards
2 Article Nominated for the BSFA Awards

The Evolution of African Fantasy and Science Fiction (2018)
Shortlisted for the British Fantasy Society Awards
2 Article Nominated for the BSFA Awards

A Shadow Within: Evil in Fantasy and Science Fiction (2019)
Nominated for the BSFA Awards

Ties that Bind: Love in Fantasy and Science Fiction (2020)
Shortlisted for the BSFA Awards

Worlds Apart: Worldbuilding in Fantasy and Science Fiction (2021)
Winner of the British Science Fiction Awards
Shortlisted for the British Fantasy Society Awards

Not the Fellowship. Dragons Welcome! (2022)
Nominated for the British Science Fiction Awards

Contents

Academia Lunare CfPs Series ... iii

Introduction - *Francesca T Barbini* ... vi

"Who Is Eru?" Literary, ethical, and theological reflections about God and Religion in Tolkien's Middle-earth
Ivano Sassanelli ... 1

Neo-Pagans & the Ainur Pantheon
Elyse Welles ... 20

A Christian Fellowship: Inklings' Perspectives on Religion, Myth, and the Word
Catherine Coundjeris ... 35

Aestheticism versus Christianity in *The Happy Prince and Other Tales* by Oscar Wilde
Barbara Stevenson ... 57

Toxic religion in utopian and cultural worlds
Eugen Bacon ... 78

An Agnostic's Prayer. The Egyptian gods in speculative fiction and Roger Zelazny
Steph P Bianchini ... 94

Darling, You're Just Divine! Queer Gods in science fiction and fantasy
Cheryl Morgan 113

"This is my story" - Girardian Theory and the Christian Subtext of *Final Fantasy X*
Giovanni Carmine Costabile 134

Heaven, Hell, and Virtual Reality
Mark Kirkbride 154

The Sacred and Profane- UFO Religions and Alien Messiahs in *Rendezvous with Rama*
Kevin Cooney 164

Contributors 179

Introduction

Humanity has been interested in answering the Big Questions of life since the beginning, and still is. Why are we here? What happens after we die? Are humans a magnificent coincidence or a divine creation? Launching a call on Religion in SFF was a way of glimpsing how SFF writers have been incorporating their views on religion into their writings, knowingly or unconsciously.

"Religion" seems to mean different things to different people. Although it generally involves ways to link humans to something transcendental, spiritual, or supernatural, there is no consensus on a fixed definition. Moreover, religion can be analysed through a broad variety of disciplines, such as theology, philosophy, comparative and social scientific studies. When I opened this call last year, I specifically did not specify the angle, as I like to be surprised by what contributors want to offer to the conversation. This is also a characteristic of Luna's CfPs, that of encouraging cross-disciplinary collaboration among contributors.

The ten papers in this year's edition are, as always with this series, varied, as we invited authors to tackle the topic from different angles to create an array of paths for leading the reader to the focussed theme. The papers are grouped in three sections.

We begin our journey in J.R.R. Tolkien's Legendarium, looking for Eru Ilúvatar (Sassanelli) and the relation of neo-pagans to the Ainur pantheon (Whaba), before looking at religion in Tolkien's own life, through the Inklings (Coundjeris). Oscar Wilde's The Happy Prince is the protagonist of aestheticism vs Christianity (Stevenson), concluding this section.

We then move on to toxic religion in the utopian and cultural worlds of Africa in the works of David Coleman and Nuzo Onoh (Bacon), followed by the Egyptian gods of Zelazny (Bianchini), for whom religion has played an important role in his writings. The second section ends with a look at queer gods from history (Morgan).

The final section is led in by the videogame Final Fantasy X, where Girardian theory make us re-evaluate the anti-religious rhetoric that has accompanied this game and its sequels since their release. The last two articles examine afterlife through virtual reality (Kirkbride), UFO religions, and alien messiahs with Arthur C. Clarke (Cooney).

I hope you enjoy them.

Francesca T Barbini

"Who Is Eru?"
Literary, ethical, and theological reflections about God and Religion in Tolkien's Middle-earth

Ivano Sassanelli

Abstract

Who is Eru/Ilúvatar? Where is God in *The Lord of the Rings*? What kind of relationship is there in Tolkien's works between Fate and Free Will or Doom and Providence? This essay tries to answer to these questions highlighting Tolkien's philological studies on *Beowulf* and his letters. This kind of analysis is essential to understand the Eru's narrative presence in *The Hobbit* and *The Lord of the Rings*, particularly in the last part of Tolkien's masterpiece in which Mount Doom is the real protagonist.

Introduction

Over the years within the studies on Tolkien's works, scholars have deepened the reflection on the religious and philosophical-theological themes (Coutras, 2016; Halsall, 2020). In this context, a question has become increasingly evident: "Where is God" within the narrative of the tales about Middle-earth? (Pezzini, 2019).

The answers to this question can be varied. For example, someone could say that God is not present in Arda and there is no explicit trace of Him. Or that even if He were there, He would still be extremely remote and, therefore, would little affect the events of Arda, especially in the Third Age in which there are no cults and religions. Or that God is a simple Immobile Engine that, narratively speaking, had only the task of starting all things, disappearing and having no longer any other role within Middle-earth (except in very special and exceptional cases).

Therefore, following these hypothetical answers, one could not—or almost always not—trace a link between the "narration" and the "presence of Eru" (or in general of the "divine") in the events of Arda. This, in Tolkien's tales based essentially on the relationship between language and literature (Shippey, 2005; Flieger, 2012), would mean that, both in *The Hobbit* and in *The Lord of the Rings*, there would be no words or concepts capable of expressing God in terms of both a *philological-logopoietic* study and a *literary-mythopoietic* aspect and, therefore, in a *narrative story*.

However the question to ask is whether all this corresponds to the truth or not. This essay will try to provide a solution not comparable to those highlighted above.

1. Eru in Tolkien's letters

The first step is to investigate how the Professor thought of Eru in the context of his *Legendarium*. What interests us to analyse here is not the development of the events narrated in the First and Second Ages but the *ratio* underlying the figure of the One, Ilúvatar, in the construction of Tolkien's Secondary World. For these reasons we will not refer to the stories of the *Music of the Ainur* and the *Silmarillion* but we will dwell on what the Professor said about these topics in some of his letters published and edited by Humphrey Carpenter under the supervision of Christopher Tolkien.

In the Third Age of Middle-earth, it was a monotheistic world of "natural theology" (Tolkien, 2017, p.220). This means that, within Tolkien's conception of the history of

Arda, there is a "transcendent God": the One, Eru-Ilúvatar. In fact, the One does not physically reside anywhere in Arda and is extremely remote (Flieger, 2002).

However, this does not mean that the One was an indifferent and immobile God, sitting on his throne of heavenly glory. He gave the themes to the Ainur to develop them through their Music and, moreover, with his "Eä" ("Let it be!"), initiated the Creation, thus becoming the Guarantor of the Free Will of his creatures.

On the other hand, Tolkien has repeatedly emphasized that Eru reserved for Himself the supreme authority to intervene, to show the "finger of God" in the history of Arda. Actually, He modified and introduced new themes—such as the creation of his Sons to counter the dissonance caused by Melkor—and, ultimately, performed what the Professor called "miracles". This happened both in the episode of the Fall of Númenor and in the desire to ennoble the human race in the cases of Lúthien and Túor.

However, Eru's intervention was not limited to the great tales and mythological deeds of ancient times: it became present also in the Third Age. The "Authority that ordained the Rules", the "Other Power", the "Writer of the Story", the "one ever-present Person who is never absent and never named", Eru had also set to work in the events concerning Bilbo, Frodo, the Free Peoples of Middle-earth and the Ring of Power.

2. *The Hobbit*: between adventures and prophecies beyond "mere luck"

For the purposes of our reflection on the presence and role of Eru in the events of the Third Age of Middle-earth, we will not analyse the origin and plot of *The Hobbit* but we will dwell only on the ending of this story that sheds new light on what happened to Bilbo Baggins. Actually, in the last chapter of this book, we read:

> "Then the prophecies of the old songs have turned out to be true, after a fashion!" said Bilbo. "Of course!" said Gandalf. "You don't really suppose, do you, that all your adventures and escapes were managed by mere luck, just for your sole benefits? You are a very fine person, Mr. Baggins, and I am very fond of you; but you are only quite a little fellow in a wide world after all!" "Thank goodness!" said Bilbo laughing, and handed him the tobacco-jar. (Tolkien, 2011, p.276)

This last scene of *The Hobbit* is fundamental for our reflection and for the understanding of its entire sequel, *The Lord of the Rings*. Words, expressions, and concepts that are used in these lines will come in handy when we will analyse the adventures of Frodo and the Fellowship of the Ring. First of all, it should be noted that Gandalf used the expression "mere luck" to designate what Bilbo's "escapes" had not been on that trip from Bag End to Lonely Mountain.

To better understand this passage, we must refer to another Tolkien's work: *Beowulf: the Monsters and the Critics* (2006b). In this academic essay the word "luck" is recalled at least twice. In fact, firstly, it is written that: "Beowulf only twice explicitly thanks God or acknowledges His help. [...] Usually he makes no such references. He ascribes his conquest of the nicors to luck" (Tolkien, 2006b, p.40). Secondly, in an explanatory note, we read: "The most Christian poets refer to *wyrd*, usually of unfortunate events; but sometimes of good [...] There remains always the main mass of the workings of Providence (*Metod*) which are inscrutable, and for practical purposes dealt with as 'fate' or 'luck'" (Tolkien, 2006b, p.47).

Tolkien, in the last lines of *The Hobbit*, through the words of Gandalf, who within Tolkien's mythology is a Maia with the function of guardian angel, wanted to tell Bilbo—but also all readers—that behind the apparent randomness of the events, adventures, and escapes of the protagonists of this story, there had not been "mere luck" but something else much greater, more powerful, and wider that went beyond the short range of Bilbo's view.

Therefore, in this story, through these simple words and through the connection between the adventures of Bilbo and "the prophecies of the old songs", Tolkien wanted to say that what might seem "mere luck" is in fact a wider dimension, a broader providential plan open to a higher Power. All this inserted Bilbo, "a little fellow" of a remote Shire of Middle-earth, into a "wide world".

And it is precisely from here that, a few years later, the Professor restarted the stories of these exceptional Hobbits, told in *The Lord of the Rings*, in a great adventure contained in the pages of *Red Book of Westmarch*.

3. *The Lord of the Rings* and the Hobbits guided by grace and Providence

In the previous section we mentioned how it is possible to trace a link between what Gandalf said to Bilbo at Bag End after the adventures at Lonely Mountain and the dialogue between the Gray Pilgrim and Frodo many years later. It is now essential to understand this link better and more deeply.

In this context, the words that Tolkien wrote in letter no. 281 of 15 December 1965, addressed to Rayner Unwin concerning the preparation of an economic edition of *The Hobbit*, are illuminating:

> Hobbits were a breed of which the chief physical mark was their stature; and the chief characteristic of their temper was the almost total eradication of any dormant 'spark', only about one per mil had any trace of it. Bilbo was specially selected by the authority and insight of Gandalf as abnormal: he had a good share of hobbit virtues: shrewd sense, generosity, patience and fortitude, and also a strong 'spark' yet unkindled. […] This is clear in *The Lord of the Rings*; but it is present, if veiled, in *The Hobbit* from the beginning, and is alluded to in Gandalf's last words. (Tolkien, 2017, p.365)

In our opinion, this text has a fundamental importance for all the arguments we will make later. What we have previously seen about *The Hobbit*—namely the fact that the events of Bilbo had not been "mere luck" but that there was something else or someone else behind them—is found this time in an explicit and declared way in *The Lord of the Rings*.

Actually, in chapter II, called *The Shadow of the Past*, what happened many years before between Gandalf and Bilbo is recalled. The place was always Bag End. This was spoken and explained once again by Gandalf. The topic of conversation was again Bilbo's adventures and in particular his encounter with Gollum and the Ring in the caves of the Misty Mountains. However, the interlocutor changed: not Bilbo but Frodo. In this chapter Gandalf says:

> 'There was more than one power at work, Frodo. The Ring was trying to get back to its master. […] Behind that there was something else at work, beyond any design of the Ring-maker. I can put it no plainer than by saying that Bilbo was *meant* to find the Ring, and *not* by its maker. In which case you also were *meant* to have it. And that may be an encouraging thought.' 'It is not,' said Frodo. (Tolkien, 2005, pp.55-56)

From this text it is clearly visible that Tolkien pointed out several times that in Bilbo's adventures there had been "more than one power at work". Actually, behind those events were: Sauron, who was desperately looking for the Ring. The Valar, who had sent the Istari to Middle-earth to counter the power of the Dark Lord of Mordor. Saruman, who wanted to become a Power and a Ring-maker like Sauron. Finally, the most important Power of all, Eru, which was that "something else at work", the Authority who, thanks also to Gandalf's help, "chose Bilbo" and now was asking Frodo to take part in a new and ancient adventure at the same time (Tolkien, 2017, p.320).

It is also interesting to note that, precisely in this context, during the conversation between Frodo and Gandalf, Tolkien highlighted the word "meant" with italics that is "intended", "thought", "wanted with intention". So both Bilbo and Frodo had been *wanted*, and therefore *thought*, in the mind of that "something else" (or "someone else") who was at work to find the Ring (in the case of Bilbo) and take it to Mount Doom (in the case of Frodo).

So, these few lines explain what Gandalf said to Bilbo when he had ruled out the possibility that the adventures of the hobbit were "mere luck". At the same time, these words had opened a world of new meaning for Frodo who, as a little creature, had found himself within something much greater, which however solicited his freedom and called him to a discernment about whether or not to accept that adventure that had already seen his uncle as a protagonist so long ago.

This is another of the essential narrative motifs in Tolkien's works. In letter no. 109 of 31 July 1947 to Sir Stanley Unwin, in response to Rayner Unwin's remarks at the reading of the first book of *The Lord of the Rings*, it is written that the

Hobbits were creatures who were accompanied "by grace (here appearing in mythological forms)" (Tolkien, 2017, p.120).

Therefore, the exceptional Hobbits had been conceived by Tolkien as characters who, because of that "spark" hidden in them, had opened up to a "grace" that, described mythologically in his stories, led them to perform unpredictable feats and that inserted them into the broader events of "world-politics", going beyond the individual good.

It recalls what Gandalf said to Bilbo at the end of *The Hobbit*. The obvious difference between the "smallness" of the Hobbits and the "vastness" of the world and the adventures to which these creatures had been called is one of the main themes of *The Lord of the Rings*. Actually, so Tolkien wrote in letter no. 163 of 7 June 1955, addressed to W.H. Auden that:

> Anyway I myself saw the value of Hobbits, in putting earth under the feet of 'romance', and in providing subjects for 'ennoblement' and heroes more praiseworthy than the professionals […]. I suppose, to speak in literary terms, we are all equal before the Great Author, *qui deposuit potentes de sede et exaltavit humiles*. (Tolkien, 2017, p.215)

Therefore, in literary terms, the Professor quoted what the Virgin Mary said in the *Magnificat*, a hymn that shows precisely the humility of the servant and the greatness of God. Here the author's attention is placed on that "*qui*" (i.e. "He"), on the "Great Author", who overthrew the powerful from thrones and lifted up the humble. In Tolkien's works, the "ennoblement" (or "sanctification") is exactly this: an *hobbitocentric* approach inseparably fused to a concomitant and unifying purely *theocentric* perspective.

This has been possible through the constant accompaniment that the "exceptional Hobbits" have received from the "grace", that here it should not be understood as "Christian" or "Catholic" but simply as the intervention of the "Supernatural" within the history of Middle-earth.

On the basis of this, it is easier to understand what Tolkien said about Frodo in the draft letter no. 246 of September 1963 intended for Mrs. Eileen Elgar in which the author, speaking of the failure of the hobbit at Mount Doom, said:

> Frodo had done what he could and spent himself completely (as an instrument of Providence) and had produced a situation in which the object of his quest could be achieved. [*But grace is not infinite, and for the most part seems in the Divine economy limited to what is sufficient for the accomplishment of the task appointed to one instrument in a pattern of circumstances and other instruments] (Tolkien, 2017, p.326)

It is very interesting what is said in this quote about the relationship between Frodo and "grace", his human and narrative path, his being an "instrument of Providence" and the divine economy and the scheme of "circumstances" that contribute to the story. This is linked to what the Professor wrote in the essay *Beowulf: the Monsters and the Critics* in which we read: "It is essential to pay closer attention than has usually been paid to the *circumstances* in which the references to religion, Fate, or mythological matters each appear" (Tolkien, 2006b, p.40).

Actually, because of his attention to detail and circumstances, Tolkien inserted the "grace" in a "mythological" form in The Lord of the Rings, especially in the events regarding Frodo and the other "exceptional Hobbits".

4. The narrative *"De vera religione"* of Middle-earth

What has been said so far allows us to understand that, although Tolkien's narrative does not present cults or religions, it is impregnated with "religious dimension". Having a divine-human relationship with the hidden but incisive presence of Eru, who intervenes at the appropriate moment making sure that the *chronos* of events become the *Kairos* of God and of the history of Middle-earth.

In this regard, both in Tolkien's correspondence and in the critical essays of the Professor, there exist some fundamental elements that allow us to shed light on this aspect. Actually, in the essay *On Fairy-stories* we read:

> Something really 'higher' is occasionally glimpsed in mythology: Divinity, the right to power (as distinct from its possession), the due of worship: in fact 'religion'. [...] Even fairy-stories as a whole have three faces: the Mystical towards the Supernatural; the Magical towards Nature; and the Mirror of scorn and pity towards Man. The essential face of Faërie is the middle one, the Magical. But the degree in which the others appear (if at all) is variable, and may be decided by the individual story-teller. (Tolkien, 2006a, pp.124-125)

And in letter no. 183 of 1956 in response to W.H. Auden's review of *The Return of the King*, Tolkien admitted that: "In *The Lord of the Rings* the conflict is not basically about 'freedom', though that is naturally involved. It is about God, and His sole right to divine honour" (Tolkien, 2017, p. 243).

From these two statements it is evident that Tolkien, as author, allowed the Mystical face addressed to the Supernatural to be present narratively within his literary works and especially in *The Lord of the Rings*. In Tolkien's last masterpiece the "real conflict" is not so much that on freedom, which is involved, but mainly concerns the "Divinity, the right to power, the due of worship" that is the very concept of "religion".

Therefore it would seem that Tolkien, around this topic, wanted to build a kind of "*De vera religione*" of Middle-earth, treated not in a theological-metaphysical or speculative-philosophical way but as a literary narrative and a historical-mythological story. This means that the "world-politics" within which the "exceptional Hobbits" had found themselves living and acting, and had as its protagonist, as the object and subject of the "essential conflict", the One whom the Professor himself defined: "the Writer of the Story", "the Authority that ordained the Rules", "The Other Power", "the Creator", "the One", "Eru/Ilúvatar", that is God.

All this is well understood in a letter already mentioned above but which should now be analysed more specifically. It is the letter no. 192 of 27 July 1956 addressed to Amy Ronald, in which it is written:

> The Other Power then took over: the Writer of the Story (by which I do not mean myself), 'that one ever-present Person who is never absent and never named' [* Actually referred to as 'the One' in App. A III p. 317 1. 20. The Númenóreans (and Elves) were absolute monotheists] (as one critic has said). See Vol. I p. 65. (Tolkien, 2017, p.253)

These words are extraordinarily important for a complete understanding of the text and narrative dynamics of *The Lord of the Rings*. In this letter the Professor had sewn the stories of the First and Second Ages with the adventures of the Hobbits and the fight against Sauron in the Third Age of Middle-earth together. This is accomplished through simple references to the text.

Actually, in these lines Tolkien talked about the failure of Frodo and the events of the Crack of Doom. To explain this, the Professor made two comparisons saying that the one who took overcontrol, or if we want who intervened, was "the Other Power", who compensated for the fact that Frodo had put the Ring on his finger. This Other Power was, at the same time, "the Writer of the Story". It is very interesting that Tolkien used capital letters. This indicates that he was obviously referring to the One, Eru/Iluvatar, who wrote and was still writing the History of that Secondary World, that is Arda.

Therefore, the Professor made a precise reference to the identity of this "Person who is never absent and never named", recalling what is written about the Fall of Númenor in Appendix A of *The Lord of the Rings*. This reference tells us that the One who had sunk Númenor was the same Person who intervened at Mount Doom: the One, God, Eru.

The only difference between these two episodes was the way of divine intervention: *explicit*, in the Fall of Númenor; *implicit*—in the manner of a "*Deus absconditus*"—at the end of the Third Age. In fact, at the time of the events that occurred in the Crack of Doom, we were no longer in the times of the great legends but at the gates of "history" and so, the presence of God, although hidden, was perceptible in the folds of the story and asked only to be welcomed by the various characters involved in the game.

This also explains the last reference made by Tolkien in the letter: "See Vol. I p. 65". This page is exactly the one analysed previously in which the dialogue between Gandalf and Frodo is told in Bag End and in which the Wizard said that there was "more than one power at work" or "something else at work".

This passage is very important because, on the one hand, it is the link between *The Lord of the Rings* and the final part of *The Hobbit* and, on the other hand, in a letter to Father Murray, Tolkien cited it as an example to indicate that he inserted God and Valar in the narrative—although not explicitly. For these reasons, we can understand that the Professor wrote a story in which Eru is present and active in the events of Middle-earth.

Actually, in our opinion, around the "real and essential conflict" that concerned "God, and His sole right to divine honour", Tolkien created a story that ties together the ancient and noble times of Númenor, the daily life and heroism of the Hobbits and the return of a long-awaited King who was hidden under the guise of Strider. Around all this, the Professor maybe managed to build a magnificent and incredible *story in two acts with an open ending epilogue*:

a) FIRST ACT: *The Fall of Númenor*;
b) SECOND ACT: *The Fall of the Lord of the Rings*:
c) EPILOGUE: *The Return of the King*;
d) OPEN ENDING: *Sam and the never-ending stories*.

5. Mount Doom and the "*Deus absconditus*"

One of the most important narrative problems that, probably, Tolkien had to face was finding a way to present the "theocentric" and "mystical" aspect at the end of *The Lord of the Rings* without an explicit reference to God but with an interaction between Eru, the *Deus absconditus*, and the story of Frodo and the Ring.

What could be the most "eloquent" sign—that it could speak with the Men's words but at the same time recount

Eru's intervention in Middle-earth—about the supernatural presence at Mount Doom?

It is very likely that, to indicate "theophany", Tolkien used a narrative device already present in Holy Scriptures: that is, the description of a fiery and erupting mountain that causes earthquakes, roars and swirls in the air. (Ex:19:16-19).

On closer inspection, this was the same situation as Mount Doom and the surrounding areas both before the Ring claimed and wore by Frodo and, more importantly, when it fell into the fire.

To this "theophany" we must add a second element: the name of the Mount. In Tolkien's works the word "doom" is used in its most diverse meanings: "fate", "destiny", "sentence", "judgment", "disaster", etc.

One of the major equivalences that the Professor used is between "doom" and "impending fate". This probably allows us to connect what is contained at the ending of *The Lord of the Rings* with the whole Anglo-Saxon tradition about the "*metodsceaft*". This term expresses a sense of disaster and death. Actually, in Mount Doom there were: the death of Gollum, the destruction of the One Ring, the Fall of Sauron and the collapse of his fortress in Mordor.

This "impending fate" had been "foretold" in ancient and mysterious prophecies told to Imladris during the Council of Elrond. In that meeting, Boromir told about a prophecy that appeared in a dream both to him and even earlier to his brother Faramir (Tolkien, 2005, p.246).

The relationship between the events of Mount Doom and these dreams allow the perception that behind that "impending fate" there was something else: a larger reality that had gone to work and was driving the events of Middle-earth.

Basically what the screaming voice of the dream of

Denethor's sons had prophesied was not the "doom of Minas Tirith" but, rather, it wanted to announce the "Doom", the "Judgment", which could not be emitted by anyone of summoned to the Council of Elrond and that it was imminent as the Sword of Elendil had been rebuilt and the Ring found. In short, the "Day of Judgment" had now come.

From all this, the connection between the "Doom" (i.e. the "Judgment", the final end of the Third Age) and "Mount Doom" (conceived as the place and time of the "impending fate") is clearer. The possibility of glimpsing this "supernatural" dimension or, as Tolkien would say, "Mystical", is also given by the place where all this happened in the story: that is the "Crack of Doom". On the one hand, in the Christian tradition it is the sound of the last trump while, on the other hand, in Tolkien's tales, it is the crack in the Orodruin crater into which the Ring of Power was to be thrown (Tolkien, 1975). Therefore this physical rift in the Mount allowed the Hobbits to become aware the dimension of the Judgment that Eru had performed on Sauron and on the entire Third Age of Middle-earth.

One wonders, however, why Tolkien wanted to insert these concepts and aspects within the final part of his literary work. The answer could be found in the essay *On Fairy-stories*, in which the Professor was speaking about an anecdote that happened to another great English writer whom he knew well since his adolescence, G.K. Chesterton (Cilli, 2019, p.55). In this episode Chesterton underlined the importance to have the Day of Judgment at the end of a fairy-tale in which justice triumphs (Tolkien, 2006a, pp.136-137).

Therefore Tolkien wanted to insert the Last Judgment in the final part of *The Lord of the Rings*, that is the "theocentric" and "mystical" part, in which justice and mercy were fully and evidently manifested.

Actually, in the events of Bilbo, Frodo and the other "exceptional Hobbits", and especially in this final part of the stories of the Third Age of Middle-earth, the Professor was able to deploy all the narrative force of:

a. what he had found written in *Beowulf*, that the manifested truth is that mighty God has ruled the race of men through all the ages (Tolkien, 2019, p.70);
b. what he noted in the critical essay *Beowulf: the Monsters and the Critics*, within God is conceived the arbiter of critical events and the *Metod* (Tolkien, 2006b, p.40);
c. what he had specified in the explanatory note contained in the essay on *Beowulf* about the fact that the *Metod* is in Old English the word that is most nearly allied to "fate", although employed as a synonym of god (Tolkien, 2006b, p.47).

Therefore, all Tolkien's philological-literary reflection on the concept of "*Metod*" and "*wyrd*" in *Beowulf* and in other northern European cultures allowed the Professor to make Eru present, in a narrative way, in the events of Mount Doom.

Conclusion

At the end of this long journey through the pages of Tolkien's works, it is necessary to tune the threads of the discourse and underline how the Professor managed to insert in his stories all that he learned from his academic studies mixed with his fictional fantasy. This is evident above all with regard to God's presence in the stories of Middle-earth: although never mentioned, Eru is present in every page of *The Lord of the*

Rings and especially in the events that occurred in the Crack of Doom.

This is more understandable if we refer to what Tolkien wrote in the *Guide to Names* about the fact that "Mount Doom" was the version in the common language of Gondor of the elfish "*Amon Amarth*". If one looks at the essay *Fate and Free Will*, they can realise that the root of the word "*Amarth*" is "MBAR" which means to settle a place and in a place, to *establish* one's home, to erect permanent buildings, to *dwell* (Tolkien, 2009, p.184). From this we deduce how "*Amarth*" carries with it both the sense of something "fixed" (such as Fate and Destiny) as well as the act of building a house or inhabiting a place.

This second meaning allows us to understand how much the category of "theophany" can be one of the keys to reading the events of the Mount Doom. Actually, while the One did not physically reside anywhere in Arda, on the other hand, during the facts that occurred in the Crack of Doom in the Third Age of Middle-earth, "the Authority that ordained the Rules", "the Other Power", Eru established temporarily His abode in Mount Doom, in the place where every other power was overwhelmed, including the Phial of Galadriel. This allowed God to take control of the situation after Frodo's failure (i.e. the *dyscatastrophe*), when all seemed lost and, thanks also to Gollum's intervention, He put end to the existence of the Ring and the Power of Sauron.

This last scene is the *eucatastrophe* in Tolkien's tale in which philology and literature, Providence and Fate have united and have given full realization to the general principle exemplified in the story and underlying all these events, namely the final part of the Our Father: "Forgive us our trespasses as we forgive them that trespass against us. Lead us not into temptation, but deliver us from evil".

This allowed Tolkien to show that divine honours are due only to God in Arda and that, although Middle-earth may appear, at first glance, as a world in which the supernatural seems to be non-existent, in reality Eru was present and acted with his powerful hand both to guide and defend the humble and simple hobbits—who have freely accepted to live an adventure—and to show the several faces of God's infinite mercy to an ignoble creature like Gollum.

Bibliography

Cilli O., 2019. *Tolkien's Library: an annotated Checklist*. Edinburgh: Luna Press Publishing.

Coutras L., 2016. *Tolkien's Theology of Beauty. Majesty, Splendor, and Trascendence in Middle-earth*. London: Palgrave Macmillan.

Flieger V., 2002. *Splintered Light. Logos and Language in Tolkien's World*. Kent: The Kent State University Press.
---, 2012. *Green Suns and Faërie: Essays on Tolkien*. Kent: The Kent State University Press.

Halsall M.J., 2020. *Creation and Beauty in Tolkien's Catholic Vision. A Study in the Influence of Neoplatonism in J.R.R. Tolkien's Philosophy of Life as "Being and Gift"*. Eugene: PICKWICK Publications.

Pezzini G., 2019. The Lords of the West: Cloaking, Freedom and the Divine Narrative in Tolkien's Poetics. *Journal of Inklings Studies*, 9(2), pp. 115-153.

Shippey T., 2005. *The Road To Middle Earth*. London: HarperCollinsPublishers.

Tolkien J.R.R., 1975. Guide to the Names in The Lord of the Rings. In: J. Lobdell, ed. 1975. *A Tolkien Compass: Including J.R.R. Tolkien's Guide to the Names in The Lord of the Rings*. La Salle: Open Court, pp.153-201.
---, 2005. *The Lord of the Rings*. London: HarperCollins*Publishers*.
---, 2006a. On Fairy-Stories. In: *The Monsters and the Critics and other essays*. London: HarperCollins*Publishers*, pp.109-161.
---, 2006b. *Beowulf:* the Monsters and the Critics. In: *The Monsters and the Critics and other essays*. London: HarperCollinsPublishers. pp.5-48.
---, 2009. Fate and Free Will. *Tolkien Studies*, 6, pp.183-188.
---, 2011. *The Hobbit. Or there and back again*. London: HarperCollins*Publishers*.
---, 2017. *The Letters of J.R.R. Tolkien*. London: HarperCollins*Publishers*.
---, 2019. *Beowulf. Traduzione e commento con Racconto Fantastico*. Milano: Bompiani-Giunti Editore.

Neo-Pagans & the Ainur Pantheon

Elyse Welles

Abstract

In this paper, I discuss the major texts of Tolkien's legendarium: *The Silmarillion, The Hobbit,* and *The Lord of the Rings*, and why these texts are seen as sacred texts by a large following of neo-pagans today. I purport that neo-pagan readers love and trust Tolkien, the narrators, and the characters so much that they don't want it to be fantasy—and Tolkien's attention to detail makes it so believable it allows them to use his fantasy religion within the construct of existing pagan beliefs.

I analyse Tolkien's background as a philologist and academic studying ancient myths, and how that enabled him to create a believable mythos and religious structure. I discuss his use of language, his writing style, and overarching narrative framework, and how the depth of his world-building in creating languages, cultures, and deep histories for his characters makes his works exceedingly believable, especially to the average reader, who is unaware of the texts or languages Tolkien was inspired by.

After viewing the perspectives that make Tolkien's books believable enough to work with as a religious framework, I explore the ways that Tolkien's created mythos easily overlays existing neo-pagan belief systems. For a modern pagan practising ritualistic worship, pantheons, and individual archetypes of gods and goddesses are interchangeable, making it easy for neo-pagans to include the Ainur pantheon in their path. The core beliefs of paganism are prevalent themes in the major texts, as well, aligning Tolkien's work with their belief system. I list some existing groups and organisations practising neo-pagan-informed Tolkien spirituality, and conclude by reminding readers that while Tolkien did not intend to create a new religion, there is a valid and significant use of his works in neo-paganism, and it is accepted by the broader neo-pagan movement.

***

Tolkien's major texts—*The Silmarillion* (1973), *The Hobbit* (1937), and *The Lord of the Rings* (1999)—are viewed by many as sacred texts; but for some, this is a literal phenomenon. In this paper I seek to uncover what it is about these texts and Tolkien's style of writing that has the power to unintentionally create converts to an imagined religion. Next, I analyse the validity of Tolkien's created mythos as a practical belief system for modern pagans, detailing how these texts exemplify the principles of existing pagan practices. Finally, examples of neo-pagan Tolkien spirituality groups and practitioners are discussed, and their acceptance within the wider neo-pagan world.

Tolkien's created world of Arda immerses the reader in more than just detailed maps, languages, histories, and fantasy creatures. Arda is a world with a religious structure so compelling it has unwittingly created hundreds of converts since its publication (Davidsen, 2019, p.33). The structure of language Tolkien used in writing his mythos is so similar to modern religious texts it convinces readers of its hidden truths, whether they be real or imagined. The Ainulindalë creation myth sets out the Ainur pantheon in its detailed exploration of the characteristics of Eru Ilúvatar and the Ainur: the Valar and Maiar he creates (Tolkien, 1973). Tolkien's highly detailed and immaculately constructed works so realistically mirror real-world religions and histories that it has built an unusually dedicated trust between readers and the source texts. The love of Arda's mythology, and its validity in the framework of modern paganism, has led to a global practice of worshipping the Ainur pantheon for neo-pagans today.

J.R.R. Tolkien was a scholar and specialist of nearly everything under the umbrella of English literature. Beyond his literature degree from Oxford, he had years of experience instructing courses on ancient languages and their literature, including Old English, Middle English, Germanic, Gothic, and even Medieval Welsh (Gilliver, 2009). When he set out to write the various stories and events of Middle-earth, he was seeking to provide a mythology he could "dedicate simply… to England" (Tolkien, 1973, p.iv), as much of the Arthurian and Celtic mythologies were incomplete, illusive, and otherwise not wholly Anglo-Saxon. Aiding him in this was his deep, unequivocal knowledge of Western European literature, history, culture, and philology—he literally wrote the book on English language when he worked on the Oxford English Dictionary (Gilliver, 2009). And perhaps most importantly, he was well-versed in mythologies across Europe. Beyond the expected Greek and Celtic studies of an academic in the United Kingdom, he specialised in Old Norse in his undergraduate studies, and was so inspired by *The Kalevala*, Finland's mythology, he set out to read it in the original Finnish (Flieger, 2017). From his lifelong study of international mythological texts, Tolkien knew what a millennia-old mythos sounds and reads like. In many ways, it was logically the next step for him to set out to create one himself.

In his studies, Tolkien observed that lasting mythologies have certain components that establish their longevity. He knew how to replicate that in his created religion to make it lasting and believable. The first necessary component is atmosphere. Tolkien recognized that good mythology was in the delivery—he depicted the stories of the Valar as ageing cultural relics. *The Silmarillion* reads like a text that began as an oral tradition passed down for a hundred generations. He understood that any mythology for England must "possess the tone and quality... redolent of our "air" (the clime and soil of the North West, meaning Britain)" (Tolkien, 1973, p.iv) and he knew how to capture that from his years of study and travel throughout the UK, living in three counties across both the north and south of England.

The text viewed most reverently by neo-pagans today is *The Silmarillion*. The most important part of a mythology is the creation story, and Tolkien begins *The Silmarillion* with the Ainulindalë, which explores how Eru Ilúvatar created Arda's Ainur, a pantheon comprised of the fifteen Valar and their servants, the innumerable Maiar. This provides the foundational beliefs for Middle-earth's civilization, particularly the Elves, and provides neo-pagan readers with a familiar type of story and cast of characters. The Ainulindalë tells us that "the music [of creation] and the echo of the music went out into the Void, and it was not void" (Tolkien 1973, p.3.) This language recalls biblical lines from Genesis, such as "and there was light" (The Holy Bible, 1986, p.2). The language of Tolkien's work is commanding and sure of itself, which the reader understands as credibility; one might believe the Valaquenta to be an oral tradition that has finally been written down.

Tolkien's writing shows an understanding of the importance of language in this task of creating a believable, ancient atmosphere, and he had the academic and professional background to implement these tools. Tolkien's translation of *Beowulf* is still used today in classrooms as the authoritative version; it is unsurprising that his own works would be able to have a cogent Anglo-Saxon flair (Fisher, 2013). Tolkien took great care to use words that had Anglo-Saxon origin (Fisher, 2013). Throughout his works, Tolkien utilised uncommon words from a Middle English glossary, such as "ye", "nigh", "aught", and "ere". This gives the works an aged feel to a modern reader—it feels removed from the real world from the start, establishing it as a world of the past.

Throughout tales of all three ages—from Third Age *The Lord of the Rings* and *The Hobbit* to First and Second Age lore in *The Silmarillion*—the narrator hints at Arda as an Anglo-Saxon past, expressing clearly that this is a world now lost, while avoiding any mention that it never existed. The narrative framework for each of the major works contributes to this mysticism and intrigue. When reading *The Lord of the Rings*, the reader is to understand that this is a found manuscript, "The Red Book of Westmarch", written by the hobbits (Thompson, 1988). This adds a layer of interest—*The Hobbit* is simply written by Bilbo from his point of view, but *The Lord of the Rings* is part of a broader catalogue of Shire events. And *The Silmarillion*'s omniscient narrator points to biblical, authoritative language, leaving no room for discussion on its truth and befitting its didactic and matter-of-fact storytelling.

When writing descriptive paragraphs of landscapes, peoples, or cultures, Tolkien's language is often poetic, and yet conversational. His writing calls to mind fairy tales of the real world, but Tolkien's tales provide a more believable backdrop than the explorations of traditional tales. Hobbits are so convincingly real, compared to fairies or sprites, that when Tolkien tells us "there is little or no magic about [hobbits], except the ordinary everyday sort which helps them to disappear quietly and quickly" (Tolkien, 1937, p.5), readers can easily believe him. This rapport of trust between the reader and Tolkien unsurprisingly leaves many readers intrigued enough to want to live in this world; and to worship his invented deities, and view these texts as sacred, is decidedly a way of doing so. It also shows a more believable foundation to neo-pagans, many of whom already believe in the Fae; they can simply add hobbits to the list of creatures they respect, from brownies to will o'wisps.

Tolkien works cleverly with assumed knowledge. Characters in *The Lord of the Rings* will name-drop Eärendil, or Fëanor, leaving it up to the reader to go the extra mile and read other works in order to uncover these characters' stories (Tolkien, 1999). This gives the books a tone of unerring consistency: the ancient, lasting history of Middle-earth feels non-negotiable; it feels like an error on the part of the reader to not know these characters at first mention, not the author's. This builds an abiding intrigue with Tolkien. It makes the reader trust what he says, he says it so authoritatively; and then decide that these stories certainly must be true, because they're both too beautiful and tragic, and too real and magical to be false. Readers of *The Lord of the Rings* often find themselves with real curiosities about Middle-earth's history beyond the Third Age, such as where Lothlorien may be today, now that Galadriel took Nenya to the West and left the Golden Wood to decay (Tolkien, 1999)—and in some ways, these questions are answered.

Having already decided to both love and trust Tolkien, his narrators, and his characters, the reader wants to learn more about Middle-earth. The structural use of the Appendices in *The Lord of the Rings* is extremely cathartic for this task. In one example, the story of Aragorn and Arwen is only found there in its completion (Tolkien, 1999). The depth of every character and storyline from *The Lord of the Rings* leaves readers with an understanding that there's even more out there, that the Red Book of Westmarch is only one account, and not the original. Tolkien explains in the Appendices that the most complete copy is found in Gondor, and that even the copies at Tuckborough and Brandy Hall "contained much that did not appear in the Red Book" (Tolkien, 1999, p.15). The historical and seemingly tangible roots of realistic characters and figures like Arwen and Aragorn being mentioned quite minimally gives a magnitude to the work as a whole—if these formidable and important characters only form a couple of threads in a long tapestry of three ages of Middle-earth, this is a culture more rich and impressive than even Tolkien could hint at. The strength of suggestion of this imagined history, beyond even the vast amount of details and deeds readers are told, provides a cultural foundation for the Ainur pantheon that seems to justify the worship and regard for Eru and the Valar.

Seeking religion is about seeking answers to the meaning of life—for explaining life's sufferings and joys, the motives and actions of people, the happenings of natural disasters and coincidences that we can't accept. Why not, then, turn to the tale of Frodo overcoming evil and all odds of failure for inspiration in times of trial? The wisdom of Gandalf, that "all we have to decide is what to do with the time that is given us" (Tolkien, 1999, p.51) can guide us, whether he was a real historical figure or not. For those who have found meaning in the text already, perhaps in the relatability of characters or in inspirational quotes, a religious adoration and adherence can be a real solace. Worshipping the Ainur is a way of creating and deepening that connection while simultaneously pursuing the answers to the challenges and mysteries of life in the experiences of Tolkien's characters.

Tolkien even tackles the question of life after death. *The Silmarillion* provides comfort for readers, as death is explained as a gift from Eru Ilúvatar to the race of Man (Tolkien, 1973). The Elves' experience provides comfort too. While at first immortality might be envied by readers, as they read they understand the cost: the unending grief of seeing so much destruction, change, and death (Tolkien, 1973). The cycle of Elves' souls returning from the Halls of Mandos to be reincarnated (Tolkien, 1973) is in line with many people's pagan beliefs as well, making Tolkien's invented spirituality fit into the existing pagan framework.

His stories throughout *The Silmarillion* can recall heroes, gods, or creatures of other mythologies—but at the same time, because Tolkien knew these existing mythologies so well, he was able to create new and truly unique characters that he knew had not been explored. Nienna is the Vala associated with grief. She mourns change wrought by Melkor, or deeds of evil committed against Arda (Tolkien, 1973). Interestingly, she does not make others sad, but teaches "those who hearken to her learn pity, and endurance in hope" (Tolkien, 1973, p.16)—in other words, empathy and emotional fortitude. There is no goddess or deity in any pantheon on earth that has these specific associations. If one needs a goddess of empathy or mourning, Nienna is a pagan's only choice.

Tolkien writes with great detail, naming fifteen Valar, their powers, specific deeds, and legends they are involved in, and which cultures and races are favoured by whom. He gives them partners and individual relationships, and shows their worship, reverence, and involvement across thousands of years of Arda's development. This lends a level of credibility to these mythologies that is stark and staggering, especially for the average reader, who would not have the background in European mythology and philology that Tolkien did. This inherently leads a reader to wonder if Tolkien discovered something—perhaps in the basements of Oxford during his over thirty years there, or by meeting one of the very few remaining Elves when out alone on a country walk. For a modern pagan to connect with deity and spiritual energy in meditation, and reach out for a personal encounter that others might not be able to replicate, is a common occurrence. It is believable then, from that lens, to assume Tolkien had done so.

The notion that Tolkien received or was relayed this information was a theory that Tolkien himself was not averse to furthering. The introduction to *The Silmarillion* is a letter to Milton Waldman in which Tolkien explains that the myths "arose in [his] mind as 'given' things," and that he "always… had the sense of recording what was already 'there'", somewhere: not of "inventing" these characters and histories (Tolkien, Letter 131). This lends itself to the spiritual messaging that neo-pagans believe in. To believe that Tolkien received a message from a higher being, a deity, a spirit guide, is common, expected, and very believable. To then explore for themselves a meditative or dream communication with Eru Ilúvatar or one of the Valar is logical from the pagan lens.

Neo-pagans believe that dreams and meditations are a valid means of experiencing deity and receiving guidance. In *The Lord of the Rings*, Frodo sees premonitions in his dreams, from Gandalf's encounter at Orthanc, to seeing both the Grey Havens and the Misty Mountains before he sees or learns of them (Tolkien, 1999). There is a decided influence of the Ring on the dreams of those it has affected, as well, in a similar way to neo-pagan beliefs in cursing or sending negative energy to others. In *The Lord of the Rings*, Eowyn has the Black Breath on her after her defeat of the Witch-king, leading her to hear "dark voices in [her] dream" which tell her of Eomer's death (Tolkien, 1999, p.868). Frodo also has "dreams of fire" as he bears the Ring in Mordor (Tolkien, 1999, p.922). But most importantly from a pagan perspective, these dreams allow the characters to make decisions and better understand what is happening—these dreams provide comforting prophecy, and 'add depth and enchantment' for readers (Schorr, 1983). These elements of prophecy and guidance in dreams would feel familiar and validating for neo-pagans, who treat dreams in much the same way.

Receiving guidance and having a deep and abiding respect for the natural elements is a core belief of neo-paganism. The five elements—air, fire, water, earth, and spirit—are attributed to each of the Valar in different ways. Ulmo is the Vala of Water; Aulë the Vala of the earth's stone and minerals; Yavanna the Vala of fruits and fertility; and Manwë the Vala of Air, to name a few simplified examples (Tolkien, 1973). In other pantheons, from Greek to Egyptian to Celtic to Native American, gods and goddesses are also assigned to different elements. In neo-paganism, a god or goddess of a specific association is entreated to for help with that which falls under their jurisdiction; entreating Ulmo for safe passage on a water voyage could be just as appropriate as entreating Poseidon.

Likewise, in an individual's practice of neo-pagan nature worship, there are different elements that one might be more connected to than others. Frodo exemplifies this in *The Lord of the Rings*, as he is often guided by air. In a dream he hears "the winds curling about the house", alerting him to real-life danger at Crickhollow (Schoor, 1983). Gandalf is tied to the fire element, as seen in *The Hobbit* by his use of fire magic against the wolves (Tolkien, 1937) and again in *The Lord of the Rings* by his defeat of the Balrog as "the Servant of the Secret Fire, wielder of the Flame of Anor" (Tolkien, 1999, p.330)—the Balrog too is of the fire element. Merry and Pippin are more connected to the earth elements, in their communion with the Ents and wherewithal to go to Fangorn amidst the fighting when the Rohirrim attack the orcs who had captured them (Tolkien, 1999). They are not afraid of the forest when they enter, despite the heaviness that Gimli had felt; in fact Merry draws comparisons to the Old Forest he is familiar with in the Shire (Tolkien, 1999). This connection to one or more elements is something all neo-pagans aspire to in their own way, and the examples seen in the hobbits, Elves, Maiar, and Valar can be understood as guidance towards that end.

The use of magic is another core belief of neo-pagans. Galadriel's mirror (Tolkien, 1999) is a form of scrying, a type of divination used by pagans. Following the phases of the moon as the dwarves do in *The Hobbit* (Tolkien, 1937) is something familiar to pagans as well, as full moons are celebrated as Esbats. Even the concept of rings containing stones and silver wrought with magical power is not unusual: the belief that gemstones and crystals have inherent magical properties is common amongst pagans, and wearing jewellery imbued with a specific power or intent is ritually practised as well. Pagans today make moon water, water that is imbued with the power of the moon on full moons, which can be viewed similarly to the Light of the Star of Eärendil being captured by Galadriel's fountain in Lothlorien (Tolkien, 1999). Broadly speaking, the prevalent theme of the pure, magical power of nature in Tolkien's works resonates strongly with neo-pagans.

Animism is a common belief amongst neo-pagans. Animism is the belief that all natural things have innate spirits, from rocks, to trees, to bodies of water, and individual places. Numina, or places of spiritual power, are found throughout Middle-earth. Fangorn Forest has a definitive power and energy to it, "old and full of memory" (Tolkien, 1999, p.491). Each tree, Huorn, and, Ent have their own spirit too. The Golden Wood of Lothlorien as well feels powerful, from the magic of Galadriel's ring but also the trees and waters. The River Nimrodel still carries the song of the maiden Nimrodel, and 'is healing to the weary' (Tolkien, 1999). It isn't just Elves who have a sensitivity to the energies: in the Barrow-downs, Frodo feels the evil before he recognizes it, much as he innately knows to trust Tom Bombadil (Tolkien, 1999). Frodo is of course an Elf-friend; but his understanding of the world feels accessible for those reading the book, when taking his life and actions as an example.

Pagans, like followers of all religions, are looking for examples of good conduct; for texts, stories, and characters to show what is right and wrong, and for there to be wisdom gleaned from these tales. *The Lord of the Rings* is at its core an excellent example of morality, reward, and the nature of evil. The majority of characters, and certainly all of those within *The Hobbit* and *The Lord of the Rings*, have a clear delineation between good or bad: no one could, or should, read the Orcs as the heroes. This is comforting and easy for readers to accept, and proposes easy-followed examples of behaviour. The good characters are ideals of action: Aragorn is the penultimate chivalric hero, while Frodo is the strong, martyring leader. Sam is a loyal follower; Gandalf, a wise tactician, leader, and motivator. These are archetypes not unlike those found in the tarot decks neo-pagans utilise. In fact, there has been a *The Lord of the Rings* tarot deck in print for almost 30 years, where Gandalf exemplifies the Hierophant, or Galadriel as the High Priestess (Donaldson, 1997).

For all of its happy endings, there is a looming understanding at the end of *The Lord of the Rings* that the defeat of Sauron is not a final victory over evil; that indeed no such victory is possible; and that balance will continue to persist. This notion of balance is a key principle to pagan beliefs. Death is not an evil, but the other side to the cosmic coin of existence in pagan beliefs. Balance will always win out to make the experience of life essentially neutral, neither wholly joyful nor painful. Critics of *The Hobbit* and *The Lord of the Rings* often say that the endings are too happy—but there is a marked tragedy, loss, and real fear throughout the texts that makes the tales feel realistic and relatable. Over fifty named characters die in those two books alone, and 'contemporary readers use *The Lord of the Rings* as a tool for dealing with death' (Amendt-Raduege, 2018). The acceptance of death, from the very Anglo-Saxon-inspired battle cry of the Rohirrim, to the willingness of sacrifice in characters like Gandalf, Frodo, Sam, and many Elves of the First Age, inspires readers towards a healthy outlook on death: a theme of new and old pagan beliefs.

Neo-pagan publications have been accepting of the Tolkien spirituality movement since the 1970s (Davidsen, 2019). Practitioners have been public since Myrtle Reece's "contact with Bilbo" in 1973, but as with most sects of paganism, the quantification of who believes what can be hard to find. Neo-paganism is usually practised "solitary" alone and often secretively (Davidsen, 2019, p.34). However, there are some groups practising openly—and even recruiting. Groups such as the Tribunal of Sidhe, founded in 1984; the Alternative Tolkien Society, active until 2005; and Tië Eldaliéva, founded in 2005, are among dozens of public and non-public groups with ritualised Eru and Ainur-based religions (Davidsen,

2019). These groups are alive and well in circles of pagan practice; articles and rituals involving the Valar are used at faerie festivals, and circulated on pagan blogs and zines (Gile, 2021). And the expanse of study, conversation, and readings of Tolkien's texts—not to mention the fairly consistent release of new publications of Tolkien's lost works—validates and encourages more converts to worship of Eru Ilúvatar and the Ainur pantheon every year (Gile, 2021).

While it is important to emphasise that Tolkien did not intend for his created mythos to subvert his own religion of Catholicism, he did intend to create a realistic mythology and imagined history that would fit for the pagan Anglo-Saxon world. In some ways the religious ardour with which the Ainur pantheon is revered is exactly what he intended. Tolkien wrote the Ainulindalë to be a creation myth for a wide history of peoples and lands. He invented Eru and the Ainur as presiding deities and powers over those peoples, with vested interest in those lands, using the professional, academic understanding he had of mythology and their structure in affecting the identity of those who believed it. Today, nearly one hundred years after the world's introduction to Arda, hundreds of people have adopted its history and taken Arda's religion for their own. We'll never know what The Professor would have thought of neo-pagans regarding his works as holy texts; and perhaps he may have feigned insult or disgust; but deep down, perhaps, Professor Tolkien may have been flattered to know he had created a mythos so easily coalesced with the ancient pagan ones he sought to emulate.

Bibliography

Donaldson, T., 1997. *The Lord of the Rings Tarot*. 1st ed. Stamford: U.S. Games Systems.

Fisher, E., 2013. An analysis of Tolkien's use of Old English language to create the personal names of key characters in *The Lord of the Rings* and the significance of these linguistic choices in regards to character development and the discussion of humanity in the novel more widely. *Innervate*, 6, pp.21-32.

Flieger, V., 2017. *Splintered Light*. Kent: Kent State University Press.

Gile, F., 2022. Monotheistic and non-ritualistic religion devoted to Ilúvatar in the real world? | The Tolkien Forum. [online]. Available at: <https://www.thetolkienforum.com/threads/monotheistic-and-non-ritualistic-religion-devoted-to-iluvatar-in-the-real-world.29799/> [Accessed 28 September 2022].

Gilliver, P., Marshall, J. & C., W.E.S., 2009. *The Ring of Words: Tolkien and the Oxford English Dictionary*. Oxford: Oxford University Press.

Davidsen, M. A., 2019. Honoring the Valar, Seeking the Elf Within: The Curious History of Tolkien Spirituality and the Religious Affordance of Tolkien's Literary Mythology. In Milon A., *Tolkien the Pagan? Reading Middle Earth Through a Spiritual Lens*, Peter Roe Series XIX. Edinburgh: Luna Press Publishing, pp.33-42.

Schoor, K., 1983. The Nature of Dreams in The Lord of the Rings. *Mythlore*, 10(36), p.46.

The Holy Bible, 1986. New York: American Bible Society.

Thompson, K., 1988. *The Hobbit as a Part of the Red Book of Westmarch*. Mythlore, 15(2), pp.11-16.

Tolkien, J.R.R., 1937. *The Hobbit; or There and Back Again*. London: George Allen & Unwin.
---, 1999. *The Lord of the Rings*. London: Harper Collins.
---, 2012. The Letters of J.R.R. Tolkien. [Kindle version] HarperCollins*Publishers*. Available at: Amazon.co.uk <https:// www.amazon.co.uk> [Accessed 30 September 2022].

Tolkien, J. and Tolkien, C., 1973. *The Silmarillion*. London: George Allen & Unwin.

A Christian Fellowship: Inklings' Perspectives on Religion, Myth, and the Word

Catherine Coundjeris

Abstract

A common religion bonded the fantasy authors: J.R.R. Tolkien, C.S. Lewis, Owen Barfield, and Charles Williams together as they shared their literary works in progress with one another in the Inklings, meeting between the late 1930's and 1949, spanning the great upheaval of World War II. The major common thread in all the Inkling literature is a stubborn search for meaning in a changing world wounded by war, plagued by totalitarianism, and haunted by modernity rife with nihilism. Williams, Lewis, Barfield, and Tolkien all share a belief in the true myth of Christianity and this is reflected in their works of fantasy. According to A.J. Reilly, "Christian theology itself springs from a "given," an experience—not an idea but a happening or a series of happenings" (Reilly, 2006, p. 6). Thus, there is room for an individual's experience of Christianity to impact the whole of that religion. Indeed, even though, each Inkling keeps his own brand of Christianity: Williams with his Rosicrucian leanings, Lewis with his conversion back to the Anglican Church, Barfield with his keen following of Anthroposophy and Tolkien with his loyalty to his mother's Roman Catholicism, they are Romantics at heart. All four men are individualists and their religion respects the individual's choices. An individual can change the direction of the world and what that individual says is important. Each Inkling finds meaning in the study of words, manifesting in their ultimate deification of the word. Language becomes crucial to the defining moment in human evolution from body to spirit.

The purpose of language and its study, culminates for each Inkling in their acceptance of the *Word Incarnate: Jesus Christ*. In their works they illustrate that the purpose of language is to facilitate human relationships and their religion does the same thing with its dogma, rules, and beliefs. The highest form of these relations is friendship and love, mirroring the relationship between God and the individual. The greatest Christian law is "to love one another as I have loved you." The greatest affirmation of his law is to lay one's life down for a friend. In Williams' *All Hallows' Eve*, Tolkien's *The Lord of the Rings*, Barfield's *The Silver Trumpet*, and Lewis' Space Trilogy the myth is told through heroes who adhere to the Tao of Christian faith. They are willing to sacrifice self for the other. We will examine the role of religion among the Inklings and the role of religion in their writing and how this religion gives meaning to their myths and, as Barfield would say, evolves the human consciousness towards a higher purpose: to love the other as the self.

Introduction

In reaction to the nihilism of the age, the totalitarian governments in Germany, Russia, and China, and intellectual societies such as the Bloomsbury Group, the Inklings—primarily J.R.R. Tolkien, C.S. Lewis, Owen Barfield, and Charles Williams—searched for meaning against the backdrop of a world struggling in a morass of meaninglessness. They viewed the world through a lens of religious belief that gave it sense and made order out of chaos; specifically, Christianity gave the universe a structure which answered the looming void of modern relativism with the understanding that there is good and evil in the world. Where Bloomsbury viewed art as line and structure and sound and rhythm, deconstructing the world down to its parts, the Inklings built worlds out of the significance of words. In fact, for them, the word was made flesh in the incarnation of Jesus Christ. Jesus elucidated the word, or truth, of God. Interconnectedness united a person with God and thus people with each other. From this bond emerged salvation for humanity, for the purpose of language was to form relationships of love and friendship to combat the encroaching catastrophe of the world. The shared religion of the Inklings, Christianity initially became known and spread worldwide through the link of friendships. In Tolkien's *The Lord of the Rings* (1065a, b, c), Lewis' Space Trilogy (*Out of a Silent Planet* 2003a, *That Hideous Strength* 2003b, *Perelandra* 1996b), Williams' *All Hallows' Eve* (2009), and Barfield's *The Silver Trumpet* (1925), the heroes of these myths struggled against the seemingly insatiable power of evil with the indestructible force of good embodied in friendship and love. "Fantasy became the voice of faith. And it made for a cracking good story" (Zaleski P. & C., 2015, p.11).

1. Religion and the Search for Meaning

After the terrible experience of World War I, and under the encroaching shadow of World War II, not to mention industrialisation and a growing cynicism among most of the intellectuals of the that time, early twentieth century thinkers came to consider the world empty of meaning. Just as the rest of the world was reeling from the horrors of technological warfare, the Inklings too were impacted by World War I and its consequences:

> Each lost friends, and each felt the guilt that any survivor of a war feels. Many of them refused to talk about their own experiences, for good or ill. Tolkien, perhaps, provides the best example. One of Tolkien's closest students, John Lawlor, recorded in his own memoir of Lewis, Tolkien, and

> the Inklings, that Tolkien never spoke of the war. "What befell him in a far-off country, wartime France, we do not know." Yet, there is much we can understand about Tolkien's experiences through his own writings and mythology. (Birzer, 2019)

Many of Tolkien's images of Mordor, the Nazgul, and the dead marshes were hauntings from his experience as a soldier in the trenches. For example, Tolkien contracted trench fever himself, and one could believe that this led to his description of the black breath that plagued Éowyn and Faramir in *The Return of the King* (1965b). The new technology of WWI, including barbed wire, machine guns, and mines, mowed down lives efficiently and cruelly, leaving soldiers with bodies torn apart and horribly mutilated. It seemed for many at that time, that God was far removed from humanity, if not in fact dead and gone. The war posed too great an obstacle to faith and optimism.

Adding salt to the wounds of this war, industrialisation came along, and uprooted the old familiar sceneries and places that the Inklings so cherished. We see this concern in all the Inklings' works of fantasy, with the overreach of science and technology taking the place reserved for God and spirit. In 1932, Lewis established a quarterly review, *Scrutiny*, which critically analysed and enumerated the ills of society, including "industrialization, consumerism, and technocracy", mourning the loss of a more idyllic view of the world (Zaleski P. & C., 2015, p.332). Tolkien hated the newly minted mechanisation of his beloved England:

> Underscored by the industrialization of Oxford, where cars now circled the dreaming spires while trees fell and factories rose in the once-bucolic outskirts. Failure to perceive the false

allure of industrial progress, he had written to Christopher in 1944, was "almost a worldwide mental disease." In this same letter (Letter 54) he drew a stark opposition between machines and art, the first attempt to seize power in the primary world, the second an attempt to create beauty in a secondary world of subcreation. (Zaleski P. & C., 2015. p.406)

Nature took on a holiness set against the evil machinations of the villains of the Inklings' myths. In Tolkien's *Lord of the Rings* (1065a, b, c), Saruman's destruction of the forests around Isengard and his decision to breed Orcs with Men to create a super Orc illustrated these evils, not to mention the wasteland of Mordor created by Sauron's lust for power. Lewis, in *That Hideous Strength* (2003b), portrayed the sinister side of science in the form of N.I.C.E.'s destruction of Edgestow, tearing down old churches, destroying cosy homes, ripping out trees and rerouting a river. Mrs. Dimble, after the violation of her beautiful country home, said, "it's almost as if we lost the war" (Lewis, 2003b, p.74). In Williams' *All Hallows' Eve* (2009), the artist Jonathan painted the beauty of the City of London and its natural elements as almost having a celestial quality that transcended the schemes of the black magician, Simon LeClerk. One of Williams' heroes, Richard, said of the painting: "It's like a modern Creation of the World, or at least a Creation of London. How did you come to do it?" (Williams, 2009, p.22). It is important to note that LeClerk looked and flinched at the painting, hating it, and advised Jonathan to hide it away and do no more of that kind of thing. He declared, "There is only one art, and that is to show them their master" (Williams, 2009, p.42). He was like the voice of bad critics who shaped art in a destructive way. Furthermore, in the first work of fantasy by any Inkling, Barfield, in his fairy story *The Silver Trumpet* (1925), told a tale of the unnatural inclinations of a princess, Gamboy, towards black arts and her misuse of nature to bring about her own purposes when she terrorised and caused the untimely demise of her sister, Violet, with a toad. Furthermore, she continued her reign of terror with Lily, Violet's young daughter, and caused the princess to have unreasonable fears of natural things of God. "Nor could she think of anything for long at a time except toads. At night she dreamed of them" (Barfield, 1925, p.41). Her unhealthy and unholy fear of nature caused her to take refuge in a tower and to separate herself from all the creatures of God. In Barfield's play "Angels at Bay" (2021), he depicted a modern newspaper editor who sold thousands of newspapers with scandalous stories to grab the attention of readers. Consequently, more and more trees were wasted as reems of paper were used to publish nothing but trash. Serakel, the Angel of the coniferous trees, lamented the pulping machine as such: "A lifeless, a sad substance that sends nothing back to earth" (Barfield, 2021, p.111). In all four works of fantasy, a dichotomy was established. Those for industrialisation were gravely in error, falling on the side of evil, and those opposed to it embodied the natural world and were seen as part of the enlightened ones connected to nature and God.

The Inklings opposed the modern philosophy that enshrined reason and pessimism while "their great hope was to restore Western culture to its religious roots, to unleash the powers of the imagination, to reenchant the world through Christian faith and pagan beauty" (Zaleski P & C., 2015, p.5). In fact, each Inkling in their own way was seeking to revive their world by retreating to what they considered solid foundations of past thinkers who still believed in the wonders of the world and hope for its future. They gave oxygen to Romantic ideals and constructs that were also religious ideals and constructs, reflecting the philosophy of such romantics as Shelley, Coleridge, and Melville.

> The Romanticism that they advocate is what Williams calls "corrected romanticism", and what Barfield means by romanticism that has "come of age"; it is romantic doctrine lifted into the realm of formal doctrinal religion and justified as being part of that religion. (Reilly, 2006, p.5).

The most important aspect of this romanticism was the strong belief in the importance of the individual, and the state of an individual's soul, thus the imaginative life of that soul became of paramount concern:

> Like Frye he sees the common denominator of romanticism as "one central and valid concept: the reconciling, synthetic imagination" with "its rootedness in a sense of the continuity between man and nature and the presence of God". (Reilly, 2006, p.7)

The Inklings' romanticism still allowed for the belief in the existence of God despite Nietzsche's 1882 work, *The Gay Science*, which declared that *God remains dead and we have killed him*. Surrendering to such a pronouncement, the Modernists either denied God's existence or questioned it to the point of disbelief. In direct opposition, the Inklings were firmly in the camp that defended the existence of God or some power of Goodness and Intelligence directing the universe despite the evidence of suffering and the preponderance of evil in our world. Atheism doubted the validity of religious beliefs because of this pain, but, according to the Zaleskis, Lewis tackled this dilemma in his theological study, *The Problem of Pain* from 1940:

> As for divine goodness, Lewis argues that precisely because God is perfectly good, he wishes us to share in his own perfect, complete and eternal goodness. God is love, and our highest bliss is to become creatures who can receive this love. But learning to love perfectly is no easy task; pain and suffering are means by which God effects this miraculous transformation. (Zaleski P & C., 2015, p.293)

In a twisted act of transformation in *That Hideous Strength*, N.I.C.E. scientists used pain as a means to control people and take away their will and their right to self-determination. This abuse of pain led to the creation of a real evil. The Belbury group resorted to breaking off from meaningful human interactions as a way of rewiring the human psyche and violating the world order, lifting to a godlike role the empty shell of a demonically controlled head. There is no love; there is no friendship: they are but a chemical response, according to Dr. Frost, one of the movers and shakers of N.I.C.E. Individuals don't matter: only the idea of an improved species. "Only one tenth part [of the body] will be needed to support the brain. The individual is to become all head. The human race is to become all Technocracy" (Lewis, 2003b, p.256). In the end it becomes clear that evil can thrive in an atmosphere where the absence of meaning causes a void where all kinds of degradations take place in the human spirit. Tolkien took us back in time, away from our current milieu of scientific discovery, to the predawn of humanity, where the struggle for the individual's right to freedom began. Although Eru, the One in *The Silmarillion*, is not really mentioned in *The Lord of the Rings*, Gandalf told Frodo that he was *meant* to find the ring, intimating that some Godlike power was guiding and protecting him.

Behind that there was something else at work, beyond any design of the Ring-maker. I can put it no plainer than saying that Bilbo was *meant* to find the Ring, and not by its maker. In which case you were also *meant* to have it. And that may be an encouraging thought. (Tolkien, 1965a, p.88)

Gandalf's service to the Hobbits and to the Elves was as a witness to the power and goodness of the One. He was a member of the Istari who were sent to aid Middle-earth against the evils of Sauron not with power, but through counsel and wisdom. Gandalf had come from Eru and spoke of Eru indirectly to Frodo. In Williams' *All Hallows' Eve*, LeClerk embodied a type of anti-Christ who had split his person into three forms and sent one of them to Russia, one to China, whilst the third remained in London with the intention of gathering followers who would lose themselves in service of this demonic being. He described his followers as such: "They aren't insects; they are something less. But insects is the nearest you can get" (Williams, 2009, p.40). The reality of a heavenly realm and a hellish one dominated all three of these fantasy worlds. Belbury, LeClerk, and Sauron reflected the depths of darkness that our own world succumbed to in the twentieth century, a depth where any dictator or black magic priest may decide to reign down terror upon humanity in their lust for power and will to dominate others. For the Inklings, a Christian outlook was the cure.

2. Inklings Belief of Christianity as the True Myth

Christianity bound these four Inklings together as much as their scholarship and love of fantasy and myth. It was this love that enlivened their faith. Though all Christians, each Inkling approached Christianity in their own unique way. It is, after all, the belief of Christianity that every individual has a special and unique relationship with Jesus Christ. All four of these Inklings considered the Christian story to be a true myth and a great story in its own right. This brings us to contemplate a walk that Lewis and Tolkien took together and an ensuing discussion:

> Lewis insisted that myths are essentially lies; Tolkien countered that myths are essentially true, for they reflect and transmit, in secondary form, the primary and primordial creative power of God…and this was the crux of the matter—that in the life, death, and resurrection of Jesus we discover a myth that has entered history. Here God tells—indeed enacts—a tale with all the beauty and wonder and symbolic power of myth, and yet a tale that is actually true. (Zaleski P. & C., 2015, pp.188-189)

Tolkien adopted his mother's Catholicism—his mother's choice had isolated her from her family; she suffered poverty because of her conversion to that religion and probably died sooner than she would have if she'd had the care of her family. According to Humphrey, Carpenter Tolkien's Catholic faith was deep and passionate, "entwined as it was with the memory of his dead mother" (Carpenter, 2000, p.76). Lewis was converted back to his Anglican faith by his discussions with Tolkien. He wrote great theological books and gave excellent apologetics on the faith. Of the process of conversion, Lewis said: "I am sure God keeps no one waiting unless He sees that it is good for him to wait" (Lewis, 1996a, p.xv). Williams, though an Anglican, was drawn to the occult. He joined the Fellowship of the Rosy Cross and also the Hermetic Order of the Golden Dawn which followed magical rites and rituals, even wearing a special robe for their ceremonies. Tolkien was opposed to this sort of thing and "distrusted Williams' fascination with the occult" (Zaleski P. & C., 2015 page 231). Nonetheless, Williams' belief in the occult lent his Christianity a magical sheen:

> The major theme of his theological work is what he calls 'substitution', 'co-inherence', and 'exchange'. As a practical way of life, substitution and exchange become a kind of physical communion of the saints by which one man may literally bear the burden of another's pain and anguish. By an act of will one may assume another's suffering, and by an act of will one may yield up his suffering to another. (Reilly, 2006, pp.149-150)

This reflects the Christian belief that "there is no greater love than to lay one's life down for a friend" (John 15:13). Barfield's Christianity was shaped by his joining the Anthroposophical fold which often put him at odds with his wife, Maud. His journey started with his "'Sophia experience', which he described as a unity with the cosmos, accompanied by certitude and bliss" (Zaleski P. & C., 2015, p.105). It led to his belief in the evolution of human consciousness, which we will discuss in the next section of this paper as it has everything to do with the discussion of language and the meaning of words. However, for Barfield, "A new version of Christianity emerged, in which Christ becomes the pivot of cosmic and human evolution" (Zaleski P.& C., 2015, p.109). Christianity was the bedrock on which these fantasy authors built their worlds. Tolkien's *The Lord of the Rings* revealed a world struggling with the fallen nature of creatures; hence, there was a good or Christian Tao that was upheld among all the free peoples of the world. Gandalf and the Elves of Middle-earth considered the dominance of Sauron to be an evil because the inviolable will of an individual was a paramount good. Gandalf taught Frodo about the nature of goodness in his council:

> Deserves it! I daresay he does. Many that live deserve death. And some that die deserve life. Can you give it to them? Then do not be too eager to deal out death in judgement. For even the very wise cannot see all ends. I have not much hope that Gollum can be cured before he dies, but there is a chance of it and he is bound up with the fate of the Ring. (Tolkien, 1965a, p.93)

Gandalf's wisdom echoed a very Christian belief that Gollum could be redeemed and therefore should not be slain. This construct actually turned out to be valid and led to the narrow path of victory for our heroes. Though Gollum remained sadly unredeemed, he did have a part to play in the end. He was the one who unwittingly destroyed the Ring of Power. Having compassion or pity for another fallen creature not only defeats the purpose of evil, but maintains the sanctity of good. In Williams' *All Hallows' Eve*, the very Christian doctrine of forgiveness brought two former antagonists together in a powerful alliance. Betty and Lester were school chums and Lester was indifferent towards her during their schooldays. When they met again, Lester was a ghost, but Betty was still able to see her due to LeClerk's magical interference in Betty's life. The two young women talked to one another and reconciled. Lester admitted, "But you may remember that I didn't behave as if I particularly liked you" (Williams, 2009, p.88). That honesty and admission allowed for Betty to forgive Lester her cruel slight. This reconciliation opened the path for a transcendent moment between the two women. Lester changed places with Betty and took upon herself the consequences and pain of the terrible magic that LeClerk had weaved. In fact, during the ordeal, Lester found herself leaning against a frame as long as a beam of wood much like the cross of Jesus since she, in Christ-like fashion, ransomed herself and Betty was saved. Betty was saved from certain death by Lester. It was an "exchange of redeeming love that had taken place between those two" (Williams, 2009, p.103). Lewis also showed this same exchange in the character of Ransom in *Perelandra* when he engaged the demonically possessed Weston in a battle, taking the place of Tinidril and Tor, the Queen and King of Perelandra, to save this world from the Fall. In fact, once this salvation was complete, Tor called Ransom "Friend" and "Saviour" (Lewis, 1996b, p.222). This exchange took on another dimension in Barfield's *The Silver Trumpet*, in such a way as to reflect the remaking of an individual. Perhaps, seeing as the princesses were identical twins, this exchange had a sense of realism to it. With the recovery of the lost trumpet, and its sounding forth, the wicked Gamboy was replaced with the kind and gentle Violet. The trumpet undid all the evil of Gamboy and she was laid to rest in the grave as Violet was raised from the dead. Violet's goodness replaced Gamboy's wickedness by the magic of the Silver Trumpet, which righted what went wrong. These substitutions all reflect the Inklings' Christian doctrine that Christ was a victim sacrifice to God and that, through Christ's suffering and death, sin was destroyed and evil conquered. Christ possesses this power because he is the Incarnate Word, the truth of God made flesh.

3. The Importance of the Word in the Inklings' Religious Beliefs

The study and delight in language is one thing that Lewis, Tolkien, Barfield, and Williams all shared, and all had illustrious careers involving the pursuit of this deep fascination. Williams worked with the Oxford University Press, gave lectures at the Evening Institute and had quite a following of students. Barfield read English at Wadham College, Oxford, where he got First Class. He worked as a freelance writer and then in his father's law firm. He was very interested in poetry and wrote many works of philosophy and criticism, including *Poetic Diction: A Study in Meaning*, his B Litt thesis, which was published in 1928. A lack of funds limited his ability to pursue academia, but he worked on various editorial staffs. C. S. Lewis, who studied English Language and Literature at Oxford University, was elected a fellow and tutor at Magdalen College in 1925. He also taught Medieval and Renaissance English at Cambridge from 1954 to 1963. Tolkien was appointed Professor of Anglo-Saxon Literature at Oxford in 1925 after having worked at Leeds University as a Reader in English Language (Carpenter, 2006, p.255-259). All four men were deeply involved in the study and appreciation of philology.

Barfield believed that words had souls. In his study of the evolution of the human consciousness, he held that words told the story of the whole human race, that they contained the DNA of our existence, mapping out all the routes we had taken to reach our present destination. In fact, for him, words took on a religious meaning as well:

> As language grows subtler and subtler, burying in its vaults more and more associations, more and more mind, it becomes to those same spirits a more and more perfect medium of companionship. In the beginning was the Word, and the Word was with God, and the Word was God. (Zaleski P. & C., 2015, p.107)

The purpose of language is to form relationships that endure and carry us through the dark ages of life. Lewis wrote a letter to his friend Arthur Greeves stating, "Friendship is the greatest of all worldly goods. Certainly to me it is the chief happiness of life" (Zaleksi P. & C., 2015, p.249). In Lewis' Space Trilogy, a philologist's skills are of grave importance. Ransom is kidnapped and taken against his will to the planet Malacandra in the first book, *Out of a Silent Planet*. His skills helped him to learn the language of the hrossa and become friends with an alien species. This friendship opened up the entire universe to Ransom and led him back to God. It is interesting to note that Ransom's Christian name is Elwin, which is Old English for Elf-friend and could be a tribute to his dear friend Tolkien. He did use such words as Númenor to describe Atlantis and thus we see evidence of Tolkien's influence on Lewis' work. The link of companionship among the Inklings was legendary and influenced their writings. Language acted as a touchstone to distinguish between good and evil in *That Hideous Strength*. During the destruction of Belbury by a risen Merlin, the followers are struck incoherent, capable of speaking only gibberish to one another. This loss of linguistic powers mirrored their devolution into creatures lacking sense and meaning; thus, devoid of their humanity. The Belbury crew had descended into the void. In direct contrast, the people of St. Anne were filled with eloquent speech and linguistic feats, intermingled with stately dancing, with the coming of the eldila, which only enhanced their relationships and their experience of joy with one another. For the Inklings, the meaning of language was a weapon against the nihilistic deadening of the human mind and soul. Williams had a way of discussing the importance of language through his villain LeClerk:

He was removing meaning itself from words. They fought against him; man's vocabulary, fought against him. Man's art is perhaps worth little in the end, but it is at least worth its own present communication. All poems and paintings may, like faith and hope, at last dissolve, but while faith and hope-and desperation-live, they live; while human communication remains, they remain. It was this that the Clerk was removing; he turned, or sought to turn, words into mere vibrations. (Williams, 2009, p.74)

According to Williams, communication was the key to the appreciation of the arts and the true manifestation of our humanity through hope and faith. LeClerk turned speech into mere vibrations, thus transforming his followers into mere insects unable to have hope or faith. We see the power of language in Tolkien's *The Lord of the Rings*. The dark language was inscribed on the Ring of Power and linked it to Sauron, its creator:

One Ring to Rule them All, One Ring to find them,
One Ring to bring them all and in the darkness bind them
In the Land of Mordor where the Shadows lie.
(Tolkien, 1965a, p.81)

It would seem that the Enemy also knew the power of Language and used it against the Good. It destroyed friendships and bonds of all kinds. In contrast, the Elvish language was light, fast, and sublime. The Elves spent long hours listening to stories, poems, and songs, and delighted in each other's company. In *That Hideous Strength*, Dr. Frost led Mark, his new pupil, to the Objective room where "Every gold of drapery, every piece of architecture, had a meaning one could not grasp but which withered the mind" (Lewis,

2003b, p.296). Just like LeClerk, Dr. Frost tore down the fabric of meaning in his victim's life to build a new obscene structure where evil could dominate the will.

The only antidote to this malaise of meaninglessness is to seek out the significance of life. Williams believed that "each of us may, in a lesser mode, repeat this divine sacrifice by bearing one another's burdens" (P. & C., Zaleski, 2009, p.261). Words and works of literature and art have meaning that bind the human race together. We are in a great communion with one another and this bond takes us beyond the boundaries of this world. There is a communion of saints that surrounds and protects us through all the shadowy realms of life. As a Catholic, Tolkien believed in the Eucharist—the Bread of life—and that in the sharing of this sacrament, one "celebrated in communion with the whole church in heaven and on earth, the living and the dead" (Catechism of the Catholic Church, 1994, p.248).

Thus, partaking in communion connects us to our deceased relatives in a great circle of unity that is as natural and wholesome as the ecosystem in a healthy rain forest. All this is possible through the means of language. Lewis's love and tribute to philology in his Space Trilogy, Tolkien's fascination with created languages in his Middle-earth tales, Williams' sense of the mystic power of words, and Barfield's belief in the soul of words, all connects to their religious constructs:

> Language is more than human speech, that it claims a divine origin and it is the means by which God created the cosmos and Adam named the beasts. As we will see, both ideas strongly influenced the Inklings, whose leading members wrote many words about the nature of words. (Zaleski P. & C., 2015, p.24)

In the Inklings' fantasy worlds this understanding gave their heroes strength to defeat evil. In *The Silver Trumpet*, Prince Peerio from the distant land of Strenvaig, went on a quest to find the love of his life: he had fallen in love with a portrait of Princess Lily. A piece of art was able to awake love in the heart of this prince. He took time to communicate with the stable boy and found out all matter of important information. After hearing of Lily's heartsickness, the prince's love took wings: he longed more than ever to marry her and to bring joy back into her life (Barfield, 1925, p.41). His arrival into the lives of Gamboy and Lily precipitated the finding of The Silver Trumpet, whose music set all things right again. The art and language of the trumpet was essential to the rule of the rightful king. In Williams' *All Hallows' Eve*, LeClerk attempted to imprison Lester's ghost within a magically constructed manikin. But her friend, Betty, and her husband Richard, recognised her voice and listened to her instructions. They followed her advice because they believed in her, returning to the home of LeClerk to free the patients within and defeat LeClerk's hold on London, China, and Russia through their love for each other. LeClerk was swallowed up in a roseal glow and he was overpowered: "He hated them, and since they held his hate, they hated him" (Williams 2009, p.175). Hate destroys and love creates. In the end, we are left with Betty, who spent her grace curing the sick victims of LeClerk. Lester departed from Richard for a time, accepting her death, and was unified with the saints of the City. In *That Hideous Strength*, Ransom, as the Pendragon, rallied Merlin's goodwill, forming a bond of fidelity with the ancient man. He reminded him of his own Christianity:

> We are in God's hands. It may unmake us both. There is no promise that either you or I will save our lives or our reason.

I do not know how we can dare to look upon their faces; but I know we cannot dare to look upon God's if we refuse this enterprise. (Lewis, 2003b, p.289)

On the other hand, the Belbury group did not encourage discussion. They offered no comfort and merely drained the individual of all reason because, in the end, the individual was considered to merely be a tool for the "macrobes." Their very humanity was eradicated and they were filled with a vast emptiness that the bent eldila could consume and use. In *The Lord of the Rings*, the friendship wrought between Samwise and Frodo on the long journey to Mordor, where they imagine themselves as characters in a story, carried Frodo to the very pit of Doom:

"'What a tale we have been in Mr. Frodo, haven't we?' he said. 'I wish I could hear it told! Do you think they'll say: Now comes the story of the Nine-fingered Frodo and the Ring of Doom? And then everyone will hush, like we did, when in Rivendell they told us the story of Beren One-hand and the Great jewel. I wish I could hear it! And I wonder how it will go on after our part.'" (Tolkien 1965c, p.281)

Sam is self-aware of the power of their story. Their deed was mythic and that myth was becoming truth for them. Indeed, this was a theory held by both Tolkien and Williams: "That myth can sometime convey truth in a way that no abstract argument can achieve" (Carpenter, 2006, p.157). The Christian myth is one where God is the Word and the Word is God and Christ is the Word made flesh. Thus, language is the mark of our humanity and our link with the divine. Accordingly, we know of God's existence through our very conversations with one another and the friendships that arise from these conversations, which actually have the power to transform us into better selves. Lewis defined this transformation as follows: "Joy, which we know as an unquenchable longing for something beyond—beyond our hopes, beyond our ken—that 'is the thing I was made for...the secret signature of each soul'" (Zaleski P. & C., 2015, p.293). I still remember when, as a ten-year-old, I read *The Lord of the Rings* and arrived at Gandalf's resurrection scene. I cried from pure relief and happiness. The moment was unforgettable for me, elevating me through Tolkien's language into a state of joy. He called this phenomenon "Eucatastrophe", which is a sudden and miraculous happy ending, despite the sorrow and failure so prevalent in the world. The hero confronts pure evil and is victorious, with the result being joyous: "Joy beyond the walls of the world, poignant as grief" (Tolkien, 2002, p.136). This joy reflects that of Christ's Resurrection in Christian mythology and the Inkling myths. *The Lord of the Rings*, *All Hallows' Eve*, *The Silver Trumpet,* and *That Hideous Strength* are all beholden to this true myth[1], reflecting aspects of its meaning in their tales.

To sum up, the Inklings, though bonded together through their mutual interest in literature, were by no means exactly of the same mind. They were individuals with dynamic energies. Williams was said to have a magnetic personality that drew followers of the occult, which offended Tolkien's Catholicism. Barfield and Lewis were on friendly terms, but also had heated debates on literature and theology. Despite this, their common binding thread was their shared religious

---

1. In their now famous Night of Addison's Walk Tolkien and Lewis come to the realisation that in Christianity: "...we discover a myth that has entered history. Here God tells—indeed, enacts—a tale with all the beauty and wonder and symbolic power of myth, and yet a tale that is actually true" (Zaleski P. & C., 2015 pp.188-189).

belief in the Christian Tao: "There is no greater love than to lay one's life down for a friend". Ultimately, they found meaning in their world, harkening back to former days of Romantic ideals, where their love of words and their strong philosophy that the history and meanings wrought within those words held a mythic quality that elucidated the mysteries of the world; that myths were, in fact, true, especially Christian mythology. For them, words unlocked the private world of the individual and bonded it with the other. This resulting unity was a joyful communion capable of toppling machinations of evil, like Sauron, Belbury, Gamboy, and LeClerk, and thus made possible the ultimate victory of humanity against the inhumanity of the evils of the twentieth century that continue to plague our world today.

Bibliography

Barfield, O., 2021. *The Tower Major Poems and Plays*. Anderson: Parlor Press.
---, 1925., *The Silver Trumpet*. [online] Available at: <www.owenbarfield.org> [Accessed on July 4, 2022].

Birzer, B.J. 2019. *World War 1 and the Inklings*. [online]. Available at: <www.theimaginativeconvervative.org> [Accessed on July 2, 2022].

Carpenter, H., 2000. *J.R.R. Tolkien a Biography*. New York: Houghton Mifflin.
---, 2006. *The Inklings*. London: Harper Collins.

Lewis, C.S., 2003a. *Out of a Silent Planet*. New York: Scribner.
---, 2003b. *That Hideous Strength*. New York. Scribner.
---, 1996a. *Mere Christianity*. San Francisco: Harper Collins.
---, 1996b. *Perelandra*. New York: Scribner.
---, 1940. *The Problem of Pain*. New York: Harper Collins.

Vatican II New Revised Edition. 1996. *Catechism of the Catholic Church*. Washington D.C.: Ligouri Publications.

Reilly, R.J., 2006. *Romantic Religions: A Study of Owen Barfield, C.S. Lewis, Charles Williams, and J.R.R. Tolkien*. Great Barrington: Lindisfarne Books.

Tolkien, J.R.R., 1937. *The Hobbit*. London: Allen & Unwin.
---,1965a. *The Fellowship of the Ring*. Ballantine Books: New York.
---,1965b. *The Two Towers*. Ballantine Books: New York.
---,1965c. *The Return of the King*. Ballantine Books: New York.
---, 1977. *The Silmarillion*, Ed. By C. Tolkien. Boston: Houghton Mifflin.
--- 2002. *A Tolkien Miscellany. On Fairy Stories*. New York: Houghton Mifflin.

Williams, C., 2009. *All Hallows' Eve*. Originally printed in the U.S.A. Oxford Reprints.

Zaleski P. & Zaleski C., 2015. *The Fellowship: The Literary Lives of the Inklings*. Farrar, Straus, and Giroux: New York.

Additional Works Read

Gunnar, Urang. 1971. *Shadows of Heaven*. Philadelphia: A Pilgrim Press Book.

Mead. M., 1983. *Owen Barfield: A Biographical Note*. [online]. Available at: www.owenbarfield.org [Accessed on July 3, 2022].

Aestheticism versus Christianity in *The Happy Prince and Other Tales* by Oscar Wilde

Barbara Stevenson

Abstract

Sometimes you have the privilege of reading a book when you are young, where the stories endure and remain throughout your life. This article argues that, by balancing aestheticism with Christian beliefs, a dichotomy Wilde struggled with throughout his adult life, *The Happy Prince and Other Tales* (Wilde, 1888) is such a book.

Aestheticism is defined as a late 19th century European art movement centred on the doctrine that art exists for the sake of its beauty alone and need serve no purpose: political, didactic, moral, religious or otherwise. It can be summed up in the aphorism 'Art for Art's Sake' or, as coined by the French philosopher Victor Cousin, 'l'art pour l'art'. The Aesthetic Movement, in which Oscar Wilde was a major figure, began around 1868, following on from the Pre-Raphaelite Brotherhood, founded in 1848 by Dante Gabriel Rosetti, John Everett Milaise and William Holman Hunt, basing their beliefs on the concept of 'Truth is Beauty and Beauty is Truth'. For the purpose of this article, aestheticism will be considered in itself to be a spiritual belief, one which Oscar Wilde not only believed in, but set himself up akin to that of being a prophet.

During the Victorian period, while continuing to expound traditional family values, churches were undergoing changes. The Oxford Movement, begun around the 1830s, sought to bring the Anglican church nearer Catholicism, focusing on aesthetics such as art, architecture, and ceremony. In contrast, the 'lower' church was keen to address social issues such as poverty, alcoholism, and crime (Jacob, 2021). This Social Gospel movement had a growing influence in the United States from the 1870/80s, coinciding with Wilde's lecture tour in the country.

Introduction

Wilde grew up in Ireland, with an Anglican father and a Catholic mother with Nationalist beliefs. Oscar Wilde himself was baptised into the Anglican Church, but later, while on holiday, his mother had him baptised as a Catholic. It can be seen from his biographies that he was strongly influenced by his parents and although he attended boarding school for seven years, he claimed to have been mainly home schooled. He arrived in Oxford from Trinity College, Dublin with his aesthetic credentials already established, thanks to acquaintances such as John Mahaffy (Ellmann, 1987, p.26). At Oxford he became a devotee of Walter Pater (Ellmann, 1987, p.46). A lecture tour of the United States in 1881/2 re-enforced Wilde as one of the main proponents of aestheticism and a society 'favourite'.

Outwardly Anglican, Wilde's religion swung between what has been described as Hellenistic paganism and Catholicism, something he focused on in his poetry. During a trip to Rome (in 1877) he was granted an audience with Pope Pious IX (Ellmann, 1987, p.70).

By 1888 Wilde had married Constance Lloyd (May 1884) and they had two sons, Cyril (born June 1885) and Vyvyan (born November 1886). At the same time, Wilde was keen to expand his repertoire to include popular prose. Both parents made up stories for their children and decided each to write a volume of children's tales. Constance's were of a traditional nature, aimed at children. Oscar wanted to produce a wider ranging work that played his aestheticism against the more acceptable social and Christian morality, marking it out in his own style. He had come to accept that aestheticism had its limitation and altered his view stating "it is not meant to express the final cause of art, but is merely a formula for creation" (Ellmann, 1987, p.249).

Although difficult to classify, for the purpose of this paper the collection will be taken to be one of fairy tales aimed primarily at children. "The Happy Prince" could be considered a fable, and "The Devoted Friend" a parable, but both retain features of the archetypal fairy tale as exemplified by the Brothers Grimm or Hans Christian Anderson: there is social evil to battle in "The Happy Prince", conflicting shadows in "The Devoted Friend" (with the Miller being the opposite of Little Hans) and cautionary advice against stepping too far outside the accepted norm in "The Remarkable Rocket" (pride comes before a fall).

The Happy Prince

Wilde's choice of "The Happy Prince" as his title for the collection, a story that unleashes a multitude of socio-political, moral and religious issues, sealed its place as the keynote story. It could be argued that "The Selfish Giant" may have been a wiser option. The more accepted morality and obvious Christian message would have made the anthology widely acceptable to his Victorian readership, but Wilde had no intention of being conventional.

As a bedtime story for children, the tale is a simple one. The Happy Prince, a youth without a name, lived a carefree life in the palace of Sans-Souci where he was always happy. We are not told how he died, yet the illustrations by Walter

Crane and Jacomb Hood, which Wilde selected for the book, are that of a young man, a prince who did not ascend the throne. A beautiful statue is erected in his honour and placed in the city for everyone to admire. Somehow, the essence of the young prince becomes embodied in the statue. A swallow, late in migrating to Egypt because of his romance with a reed that ultimately failed, stops to shelter under the statue. The statue is crying and when the swallow asks why, the Happy Prince tells him of the suffering he can see in the city, which he was unaware of when alive. He asks the swallow to deliver the ruby from his sword to a woman whose son is ill. The swallow complies, but the Happy Prince continues to ask him to stay a little longer and distribute the rest of his jewels and gold leaf to the poor until the statue is bare and blind due to giving away his sapphire eyes. The swallow decides to stay with the Happy Prince, because he can no longer see. Eventually, because of the cold weather, the swallow dies, but before he does so he gives the Happy Prince a kiss, which breaks the statue's heart. The town council decides that the statue is too ugly for public display and it is melted down, apart from the lead heart which refuses to melt. The heart and the body of the swallow are thrown away, but God rewards them by receiving the swallow and the Happy Prince into paradise.

The story appears to be an aesthetic one of outer and inner beauty, some claim foreshadowing Wilde's novel *The Picture of Dorian Gray* (Wilde, 1891), but it also raises questions about society and its priorities, bringing in the Christian message of giving to the poor. Considering it from an aesthetic point of view, the palace and gardens of Sans-Souci are outwardly beautiful. The Happy Prince lives a shallow life, happy for happiness' sake. The statue is outwardly beautiful and its only purpose is to be so, fulfilling the aesthetic view of art for art's sake. A mother asks her son why he can't be like the Happy Prince and a passer-by mutters he is glad someone in the world can be happy. (Wilde, 1888, p.5)

The choice of a swallow as the prince's companion is not merely because it is a migratory bird. Swallows have long been a religious symbol in Western art and literature. George Ferguson writes in *Signs and Symbols in Christian Art* that the swallow is a common symbol in paintings of the Italian Renaissance—a period with which Wilde was familiar—signifying the incarnation of Christ (Ferguson, 1961). In Greek mythology, the swallow is seen as a bringer of luck, love and happiness, being associated with the goddess Aphrodite. (Lederer, 2019). In the story, the swallow regales the prince with stories of the wondrous sights he has seen in far off lands: red ibises on the Nile, green snakes that are fed honey-cakes and so forth. (Wilde, 1888, p.15)

Being happy is not the same as feeling happy. Although the statue will always be known as the Happy Prince, when the swallow shelters at its feet, the statue is crying. It is here that Wilde moves the story from one of aestheticism, to one seeking to raise a socio-political issue, highlighting the inequality in society. Although the Happy Prince's intentions are good, one can question the usefulness of his actions. By giving his wealth to a small minority of the poor, he denies the greater majority the joy of appreciating his beauty. For example the Charity Children love the statue because the Happy Prince looks just like an angel (Wilde, 1888, p.5). When the statue is bare, it serves no purpose and is regarded as an eyesore. The notion that poor people do not appreciate beauty and that public money should only be spent on utilities such as schools and hospitals is one that persists in certain areas of society today. Perhaps to counter this attitude, Wilde has the young match girl remark "what a lovely bit of glass", appreciating the sapphire for its beauty, unaware of its monetary value (Wilde, 1888, p.14). This may be seen as part of Wilde's struggle with aestheticism and Christian beliefs. Is the happiness inspired by the statue in its original state of more or less value than relieving the misery of a small number of individuals? The story gives no definitive answer—it is left for the reader to ponder.

It should be noted that despite making his social points and highlighting the darker side of beauty, where poverty, inequality and exploitation are used to support the decadence of a few—for example the poor seamstress embroidering a satin gown for a maid-of-honour to wear at a court ball (Wilde, 1888, p.9)—Wilde surrounded himself with aesthetically beautiful things and it is here we can sense some of the dichotomy. In his biography of Oscar Wilde, Richard Ellmann tells how a gift of £50 from an aunt, intended to help him and his wife begin their married life, was used to buy two Apostle spoons, much to his aunt's disgust (Ellmann, 1987, p.240). The family also had a butler, who, according to his son, Vyvyan Holland, slept in an alcove tucked away somewhere between the second and top floor of their house (Holland, 1954, p.48).

Considering the story from a religious viewpoint it may be assumed that the Prince was acting in accordance with the Christian message when, like St. Francis of Assisi, he gave everything he had and embraced poverty (Moorman, 1977, pp.81-85). It is made plain, though, that this is not the path for everyone. In the Gospels, Jesus instructs the rich man to sell everything he has and give to the poor (Matthew, 19:21) (Mark, 10:21), but adds *"then come, follow me"*. The man is promised greater rewards in heaven in return. The test is one of faith, more than poverty. The believers in the infant church sold their possessions and gave to those in need (Acts 2:44). However, in contrast, when the disciples chided the woman for anointing Jesus with expensive perfume that could have been sold and the money used to help the poor, Jesus berates them and accepts the gift (Matthew, 26:6-13) (Mark, 14:3-9) (John, 12:3-7). In the parable of the Good Samaritan, the Samaritan helps the stricken traveller, but not at the expense of bankrupting himself (Luke, 10:33-35). The issue, as Wilde realised, is not a straight forward one and the happy-ever-after ending for the Happy Prince and the Swallow reflects this. The swallow and Happy Prince are taken to Paradise, where they enjoy a carefree existence of love and harmony, without having to consider human suffering, which seems like being back in Sans-Souci.

So what is it about "The Happy Prince" that raises it above other Victorian stories of morality and philanthropy and transforms it into an enduring classic? I would put forward the idea that it is the relationship between the Happy Prince and the swallow and in particular their final kiss. The swallow is initially cajoled into staying one night to aid the Prince in assuaging his own guilt, but this develops into true love.

As both the swallow and the Happy Prince are male, and the kiss is on the lips, some critics claim an element of homosexuality, however the story is about a bird and a statue and I believe Wilde intended the love to transcend categorisation. The reader may be reminded of the kiss between the dying Lord Nelson and Thomas Hardy after Trafalgar. Although it has been propounded that the phrase was misheard and should have been "Kismet, Hardy" rather than "Kiss me, Hardy" the fact that the kiss was given was witnessed by three people on board the ship—Chaplain Alexander Scott, surgeon William Beatty and purser Walter Burke (Greenwich, n.d.).

The kiss is reminiscent of that in Friedrich Schiller's ode "An die Freude" (To Joy) written in 1785 and published in 1786 (Schiller, 1786) which was used by Beethoven in his Ninth Symphony (Beethoven, 1824). Beethoven uses the line "Diesen Kuß, der ganzen Welt" (this kiss to the whole world), speaking of universal brother/sisterhood.

In passing, we can consider the kiss offered to Jesus by Judas Iscariot in the garden of Gethsemane—an act of betrayal. The arresting party needed someone to identify Jesus in the dark. The guards did not insist on a kiss. Any sign would have sufficed. Jesus himself asked '*why a kiss?*' according to Luke's gospel (Luke 22:48). There are many theories (Massie, 2005), for which the reader is referred to Further Reading. Suffice to point out the special nature of a kiss. In Wilde's story, it is the kiss of the dying swallow that breaks the Happy Prince's heart—an outward show of their deep spiritual love. Wilde manages to avoid oversentimentality at this point by adding the aside that "it certainly was a dreadfully hard frost" (Wilde, 1888, p.17) making the moment a poignant one, revealing the true inner beauty of both the statue and the swallow.

The Selfish Giant

According to his son Vyvyan, in *Son of Oscar Wilde* (1954), "The Selfish Giant" made his father cry when reading it. When his brother Cyril asked him why, Oscar Wilde replied that 'really beautiful things always make me cry' (Holland, 1954, pp.53-54). Walter Pater claimed that the story was "perfect in its kind" (Ellmann, 1987, p.282).

Vyvyan was one and a half when the story was originally

published, and his brother Cyril was three. Both were too young to appreciate the story fully, but along with the others in the collection, it was intended to be read aloud to children in the Irish story-telling tradition Wilde was brought up with. This includes the listener in the tale and avoids what otherwise could come across as pulpit preaching. The Giant's garden is taken by numerous reviewers to be the Garden of Eden, with mankind being cast out, and allowed to re-enter by way of the Christ child. The child in the story carries the stigmata so that the reader is in no doubt who he represents. However the analogy of the Garden of Eden can only be adhered to at a general level. The garden belongs to the Giant and he is the one who casts the children out, but he is not God.

It isn't unreasonable for an adult to want privacy in their garden, but the story is for children, therefore Wilde, as the storyteller takes the side of the children. The reader is reminded of Jesus rebuking the disciples for dismissing the children with the words "Suffer the little children to come onto me" (Mark 10:14-15).

At the end the child/Christ tells the Giant "today you shall come with me to my garden, which is Paradise" bringing to mind the words of Jesus to the repentant thief on the cross (Luke 23:43).

In this tale, there is no conflict between aestheticism and Christianity. Wilde is able to bridge the dichotomy by allowing aesthetic details to set the scene. He uses all the senses to draw the reader into the alluring garden, with phrases such as "soft, green grass" (touch), "beautiful flowers like stars" (sight), "twelve peach trees that in the spring time (sic) broke out into delicate blossoms of pink and pearl" (smell), "in the autumn bore rich fruit"(taste) and "birds...sang so sweetly" (sound) (Wilde, 1954, p.30). The petals of peach blossom are reputed to be able to put people into an intense trance of love and in Taoism the peach tree symbolises longevity and immortality.

The Nightingale and the Rose

The elements of a fairy tale are in place: the hero, the seemingly impossible quest, the shadow element and the moral. The theme is one of romantic love—although as in many fairy tales this is little more than lust which we can kindly call infatuation. Wilde gives it a 'modern' twist by the girl not being 'won' by the man bearing a flower. She comes across as fickle and materialistic, but this is unfair, as she is not aware of the nightingale's sacrifice. The story deals with a student who falls in love with the professor's daughter. She will not go with him to the ball unless he brings her a red rose. The only rose bush in the garden that can give red roses has been damaged by storms and cold weather and has no flowers. The nightingale, inspired by her own romantic nature, asks the rose how she can get a flower. The answer is by piercing her heart with a rose thorn and singing all night while her blood drains into the bush. "What is the heart of a bird compared to the heart of a man?" (Wilde, 1888, p.23).

The bird forces a thorn into her body and sings. Finally, when the thorn enters her heart, and the bird dies as a result, the rose turns red with the sacrificial blood. The student takes the rose, without appreciating the nightingale's sacrifice, but it is not good enough for the girl, who prefers jewels from the chamberlain's son. Materialism over sacrifice. The rose is discarded and the student goes back to his studying. Logic being more useful than love.

It may be thought on a simple level that the nightingale's death was in vain, but she was not forced, or even asked, to make the sacrifice. She chose to do so from free will, keeping faith with her notion of love and romance. Love for the sake of love. The rose was an aesthetic and symbolic embodiment of this—and can be compared to a work of art. Many artists claim to put their life into their work, although perhaps not so literally.

In a letter to a friend Wilde wrote:

> The nightingale is the true lover, if there is one. She, at least, is Romance, and the Student and the girl are, like most of us, unworthy of Romance. [...] I like to fancy that there may be many meanings in the Tale—for in writing it [...] I did not start with the idea and clothe it in form, but began with a form and strove to make it beautiful enough to have many secrets and many answers. (Wilde, 1888b)

Wilde concurs with the artistic view at that time of a natural symmetry, or shadow, between love and sacrifice. In his prose poem "The Master" (Wilde, 1894) he reverses the theme, with a young man complaining that although he has worked miracles, he has not been crucified like Christ.

Although the student claims to want the girl's love, he does nothing himself to gain it. He believes getting the rose is impossible therefore he bewails his bad luck/fate without trying to over-ride it. There is no apparent sacrifice on his side, therefore no love, although it may be argued that giving up the love of a person for the love of philosophy is a form of sacrifice.

From an aesthetic point of view, love equates with beauty that equates with truth. The poet John Keats wrote "Truth is beauty, beauty truth" (Keats, 1819). This is closely linked to the Trinity of the church. Truth being God the father, Love being Jesus and Beauty being the Holy Spirit.

The nightingale sings of the love perfected by death, and she is prepared to put her words into actions. Her gift is selfless and her death, (a thorn in its heart) reminds the reader of the crown of thorns Jesus wore on the cross, linking the two sacrifices (Matt 27:29; Mark 15:17; John 10:2). It is perhaps inappropriate, though, to compare the death of the nightingale to that of Christ. The nightingale's sacrifice was for her belief in romantic love, which was aesthetic in origin, whereas according to Christian doctrine, Jesus' sacrifice was for the salvation of mankind. The story, therefore, is one of aestheticism rather than Christianity.

The Devoted Friend

On the surface, "The Devoted Friend" is a simple story teaching children what makes a good friend. However, in the world of Oscar Wilde, things are never straightforward. The story begins with a water rat, a mother duck and a linnet discussing the nature of friendship. The water rat declares that he "should expect my devoted friend to be devoted to me" (Wilde, 1888, p.38). To which the linnet responds by asking what he would do in return, thus raising the question of whether friendship can only exist in an environment of mutual give and take. Friends help one another. The linnet then tells the story of Little Hans and the Miller.

The Miller (sic), a self-declared man of noble ideals, declares himself to be a devoted friend to Little Hans and Hans is proud to have him as such. However, it is clear that the Miller is using Hans, giving nothing in return except the promise of a broken wheelbarrow, which is never fulfilled. Hans cannot afford to give the wealthy Miller his possessions, but when he voices his concerns the Miller accuses him of not being a true friend. The story ends with poor Hans going to fetch the doctor for the Miller's son on a wild, stormy night. Hans does not have a lantern and the Miller does not give him his. Hans is able to reach the doctor, but on the way home he falls into a pool of water on the moor and drowns. The Miller takes his place as chief mourner, bemoaning the fact that he is now left with a broken wheelbarrow to get rid of. At Oxford, Wilde, an admirer of John Ruskin, had humorously said that he had enjoyed the distinction of filling Ruskin's "especial wheelbarrow" (Ellmann, 1987, p.48) and he may have been thinking of that when he chose a wheelbarrow as the object of the Miller's gift.

Despite the Miller's fine talk of being a devoted friend, he seems to be no friend to Hans at all, and Little Hans' devotion to the Miller is ludicrously misplaced. The water rat asserts that a devoted friend is someone devoted to the recipient, expecting nothing in return. As the Miller puts it "Flour is one thing and friendship is another, and they should not be confused." (Wilde, 1888, p.41).

The theme of friendship is a common one for writers, so what makes Wilde's story stand out?

It may be the question of who the devoted friend of the title is. The Miller claims he is a devoted friend to Little Hans, but his actions speak otherwise. Hans shows he is a devoted friend to the Miller, although he does not claim such a lofty title. The story encourages the reader, or listener in the case of younger children, to consider friendship in a deeper vein. What actually constitutes friendship and who is fit to judge a relationship? We are told that Hans had many friends—and indeed his funeral was well attended—yet no-one visited him in winter or offered him aid, so could they be considered true friends? It may be that at some point, the Miller would have proven a modicum of friendship by off-loading his broken wheelbarrow onto Hans. Wilde may have been thinking of a childhood incident when he wrote the story. He had given his brother his teddy bear, but whenever he was angry with him, he would threaten to reclaim the bear (Sturgis, 2018, p.16).

Typically, the story is crammed with aesthetic images. A paragraph is given over to describing the beautiful and seemingly exotic flowers growing next to more common flowers in Hans' garden: among them Damask Roses, Fair-maids of France and the Flower-de-Luce. Wild Basil, Cowslips and Ladysmock.

The characters have witty, but pointless debates, as between the water rat, mother duck and linnet, or the Miller, his wife and their young son, showing off some jewels in Wilde's repertoire. Young readers would probably not understand all the humour, but the water rat has a wonderful line advising that the duck's disobedient children should be drowned. This seems a little harsh, yet one can imagine parents reading this at bedtime and making a joke of it perhaps by adding their own ad libs. The fact that the story has a moral, sends the water rat into apoplexy. Aestheticism offers no answers to the questions on friendship, and does not wish to.

What of Christianity?

The linnet's story can be seen as a parable in a similar vein to those told by Jesus. The water rat and duck being unable to see beyond their own narrow-mindedness. The church comes in for some gentle mocking. The Miller's wife flatters her husband by saying "The clergyman himself could not say such beautiful things as you do, though he does live in a three-storied house, and wears a gold ring on his little finger" (Wilde, 1888, p.40), but what does the Bible, specifically the New Testament and Jesus himself, have to say?

Jesus tells his disciples that a true friend is willing to lay down his life for his friend. "Greater love has no man than this, that he (sic) lay down his life for his friends" (John 15:13). Jesus goes on to deliver on this, although his sacrifice is not only for his friends, but for all mankind. "And he died for all, that those who live should no longer live for themselves, but for him who died for them" (2 Cor 5:15).

Jesus' idea of friendship is not unconditional. In John's gospel, Jesus goes on to say: "You are my friends if you do what I command" (John 15:14). This seems to be the Miller's understanding of friendship, with Hans being his disciple. He (the Miller) believes he is intellectually, spiritually, and socially above Hans. It can be noted that in the Bible there is no suggestion of Jesus reciprocating and doing what his disciples command, because he is their leader, yet as a friend he listens to/and acts upon their concerns. Jesus is willing to die for his friends—something the Miller would not do.

The Miller claims to be "a devoted friend", which is his way of exploiting Hans. He promises Hans a broken wheelbarrow, but doesn't give it to him. When the Miller asks Hans to give him flowers and a plank of wood, Hans makes excuses at first, but accedes. This is similar to Jesus' parable of the two sons (Matt 21:28-32), where a father asks his sons to work in the vineyard. The first says he won't, but later does, while the second son says he will, but doesn't.

Friendship would seem not to have any hard and fast rules. Readers can decide for themselves what constitutes a relationship and whether they reach a definitive solution or not is immaterial. I believe what raises Wilde's tale from the myriad of stories about true and false friends, is neither based on aesthetics nor Christianity. It is simply the tag line—A devoted friend is devoted to me. Who would not want such a friend, devoted to them without conditions?

The Remarkable Rocket

This is arguably the most aesthetic story in the collection, and with a reduced Christian content, it is the one most representative of Wilde's wit. It begins with an indulgent description of the King's (sic) son, a youth with dreamy violet eyes and hair like fine gold, meeting his bride-to-be for the first time. She is a Russian Princess (sic), who had driven from Finland in a sledge shaped like a great, golden swan and drawn by six reindeer. The marriage celebration is to be a grand affair and a firework display has been planned for the finale (Wilde, 1888, pp.54-71).

So far, so good, as a bedtime story for children goes. The narrative then switches to a discussion among the fireworks. Wilde over-indulges in clever conversation and seems to parody himself, taking on the role of the rocket, who is not only full of himself, but has, as the Catherine Wheel observes, a truly romantic nature. He tells the other fireworks, "I am a very remarkable Rocket, and come of remarkable parents" (Wilde, 1888, p.59). This was true of Wilde, whose father Sir William Wilde was an eminent surgeon, writer, folklorist and natural historian and whose mother "Speranza" was a celebrated poet in Ireland (Holland, 1954, pp.17-19). Just as, anecdotally, Wilde declared his genius at US customs in 1882 (Martin, n.d.), the rocket boasts of his magnificence. Having been moved to tears by one of his own imaginings, though, he is too damp to go off with the other fireworks, come the display. The next day he is thrown over the wall of the palace garden into a ditch.

It has been argued by various reviewers that while gently mocking himself, Wilde is also taking a more vicious swipe at the artist Whistler, whom he saw as being vain and narcissistic (Sturgis, 2018, p.348). Indeed, the rocket bears some resemblance to Malvolio in Shakespeare's *Twelfth Night*, prancing around in his yellow stockings (Shakespeare, 1601-1602).

Without making a grand point of it, Wilde also takes the opportunity to illustrate how easily people with authority discard anyone who is unable to be of use to them. However, the rocket refuses to be suppressed and does not believe he has failed. He has faith in himself and knows that he will be appreciated in due course. He declares that he is destined to be a sensation in the world, but nobody listens to him. When the rocket does finally go off, thanks to two little boys who put him on their pile of faggots to make a fire to boil their kettle, the boys are asleep and nobody sees or hears him.

The story, despite being full of witty quips and one-liners that are unlikely to be appreciated by children, superficially has a Sunday school moral: pride is a sin. The big-headed rocket is not as great as he believes himself to be and subsequently fails in his mission to impress. From numerous sources, including Sunday school songs of the time, children were taught that humility is a virtue and putting oneself down is the norm. This topic to too large to expand upon here, but one need only think of songs such as *Jesus Loves Me* with the lyrics "Little Ones to Him belong, They are weak, but He is strong" (Warner, 1859) or *Take Me As I Am* with lyrics such as "Helpless I am and full of guilt" (Hamilton, 1860). The hymnologist and musicologist J R Watson commented in *The English Hymn* that such-like songs were "manipulative… regressive and infantile… in danger of becoming complacent with no room for doubt or thought" (Watson, 1999, pp.492-493; Clarke, 2016, p.110).

Similar instances of Victorian morality linger in Britain today, with sections of society eager to shoot down anyone who strives to be more than is expected of them. These critics often believe themselves pious in doing so. The rocket could have been considered confident, if overly so, and encouraged in his endeavour. The others could have been, if not happy for him, at least accepting of his faults. Instead he was disregarded as being boastful and narcissistic, traits which many of the other characters in the story also had. Oscar Wilde himself was surrounded by contemporaries eager to disapprove of and mock his clothing, lifestyle and mannerisms, for no justifiable reason other than personal dislike (and possibly jealousy). He had made people heartily sick of the words "'beauty' and 'beautiful'" (Ellman, 1987, p.200).

Being judgemental is not the Christian message. In fact it could be said to be the opposite of it. What right do others have to criticise? When faced with the adulterous woman, Christ challenged those without sin to throw the first stone (John 8:7). He also warned against hiding your light under a bushel (Matt 5:15; Mark 4:21; Luke 11:33).

By staying true to the conviction of his own worth, the rocket rose above the petty negativity of his fellow fireworks and the creatures on the other side of the wall. The fact that no-one saw him is inconsequential. In his head he was brilliant and he didn't listen to anyone criticising him. When one of the boys described him as an "old stick" he convinced himself the boy had said "gold stick" (Wilde, 1888, p.70).

I would argue that in this story, it is the aesthetic view that appeals to the reader. Nobody in the story has any real concerns. The prince and princess have a fairy tale romance in a beautiful palace. The fireworks, although squabbling, are happy with themselves, as are the creatures in the ditch. The over-large, pompous nature of the rocket is irritating, but reflects his opinion of himself, and his stance against mediocrity and false modesty should and is infinitely better than the toe-curling hypocrisy of characters such as Uriah Heep in Dickens' David Copperfield (Dickens, 1850).

That, I believe, is what makes the rocket, and the story, truly remarkable.

Conclusion

Oscar Wilde's flamboyant nature and witty quips often concealed the complexity of his character. An article of this nature can only touch on the spiritual issues running through his work. It can be concluded, though, that by intertwining his belief in Aestheticism and his Christian upbringing, he was able to achieve a satisfactory balance in the stories.

Aestheticisms gives us *art for art's sake* and the book was deliberately aesthetic in its outer appearance, with carefully selected illustrations and cover design (Sturgis, 2018, pp.363-364). Christianity demonstrates *love for love's sake*. The five stories reflect different aspects of love: socio-political love for fellow men ("The Happy Prince"), Christ's love ("The Selfish Giant"), friendship ("The Devoted Friend"), romantic love ("The Nightingale and the Rose") and self-love ("The Remarkable Rocket").

In the Bible, Jesus tells his followers "unless you change and become like little children, you will never enter the kingdom of heaven." (Matt 18.3) The critic Owen Dudley Edwards amended this to read "unless we be as little children we shall never fully enter the kingdom of Oscar Wilde" (Edwards, 2003 p13).

A sentiment, when contemplating *The Happy Prince and Other Tales*, that is extremely apt.

Bibliography

Beethoven, L., 1824. *Ninth (Choral) Symphony*. Vienna: s.n.

Clarke, M., 2016. *Music and Theology in Nineteenth Century Britain*. s.l.:Routledge.

Dickens, C., 1850. *David Copperfield*. London: Bradbury and Evans.

Edwards, O.D., 2003. *The Stories of Oscar Wilde: The Complete Works of Oscar Wilde*. s.l.:Harper Collins.

Ellmann, R., 1987. *Oscar Wilde*. London: Hamish Hamilton Ltd.

Ferguson, G., 1961. *Signs and Symbols in Christian Art*. Oxford: Oxford University Press.

Greenwich, R. M. o., n.d. *Royal Museums Greenwich*. [Online] Available at: <https://www.rmg.co.uk/stories/topics/what-were-nelsons-last-words> [Accessed 7 July 2022].

Hamilton, I.D.S.a.E., 1860. *Take Me As I Am*. s.l.: s.n.

Holland, V., 1954. *Son of Oscar Wilde*. 2nd ed. London: Rupert Hart-Davis.

Jacob, W.M., 2021. *Religious Vitality in Victorian London*. Oxford: Oxford University Press.

Keats, J., 1819. *Ode to a Grecian Urn. Annals of the Fine Arts*. Accessed online, numerous sources.

Lederer, R., 2019. *ornithology.com*. [Online] Available at: <https://ornithology.com/swallows-and-tattoos/>. [Accessed 7 July 2022].

Martin, G., n.d. *The phrase finder*. [Online] Available at: <https://www.phrases.org.uk/meanings/191400.html> [Accessed 28 June 2022].

Massie, A., 2005. *In Defence of Judas*, s.l.: The Independent. www.independent.co.uk. [Online] Available at: <https://independent.co.uk/news/uk/this-britain/in-defence-of-judas-529878.html> [Accessed 21 July 2022].

Moorman, J.R.H., 1977. *Richest of Poor Men*. 1982 ed. London: Darton, Longman and Todd Ltd.

Schiller, F., 1786. *An die Freude*. Germany: Thalia.

Shakespeare, W., 1601-1602. *Twelfth Night or What You Will*. s.l.:s.n.

Sturgis, M., 2018. *Oscar A Life*. London: Head of Zeus.

Warner, A.B., 1859. *Jesus Loves Me*. s.l.: s.n.

Watson, J.R., 1999. *The English Hymn: A Critical and Historical Study.* quote taken from Music and Theology in Nineteenth Century Britain edited by Martin Clarke (Routledge 2016) ed. Oxford: Oxford University Press.

Wilde, O., 1888. *The Happy Prince and Other Tales*. London: s.n.
---, 1888b. Letter to a friend, May 1888. Accessed online Anon., 2021. *interestingliterature.com*. [Online] Available at: <https://interestingliterature.com/2021/06/oscar-wilde-the-nightingale-and-the-rose-summary-analysis/> [Accessed 2 Aug 2022]
---, 1891. *The Picture of Dorian Gray*. shorter version originally published in Lippincott's monthly magazine, July 1890. Vol 46 no 271 pp3-100 ed. London: s.n.
---, 1894. *The Master*. The Fortnightly Review.

Further Reading

Linklater, E., 1939. *Judas*. London: Jonathon Cape.

Wilde, W., 1867. *Lough Corrib: It's Shores and Islands*. Dublin: McGlashan and Gill.

Toxic religion in utopian and cultural worlds

Eugen Bacon

Abstract

> The witch doctor observed the young girl as she approached. The large clay pot on her braided head was heavy with water, and her exposed breasts were decorated with white-black drawings in intricate patterns. The girl's long, thin legs seemed too fragile to bear both her broad hips and water-laden pot as she navigated the steep hill that jutted out of the desolate landscape like a mottled boil.
> —*A Dance for the Dead* (p.3)

Religion is largely the belief in, worship or adulation of, one or more superbeings or controlling powers that may be a deity such as a spirit, god or goddess. In utopian fiction, religion manifests itself in belief and commitment to a people or an ideology. In African mythology, the spirit world and realms of the dead may come into play, with a witchdoctor as the conduit between the faithful and the deity—evidenced in British-Nigerian author Nuzo Onoh's adoption of African spirituality in her fiction. It so happens that an individual or a collective may exploit societal faith, with devastating consequences. This essay looks at what religion is, how it manifests itself, 'why religion?', and abuse in religion, with exemplars in three expertly-crafted narratives on toxic religion in utopian and cultural societies: David Coleman's short story "The Shaming", and Nuzo Onoh's works—her short story "Ogali" and novel *A Dance for the Dead*.

What is Religion?

The exploration of religion in science fiction or epic fantasy is generally not in its own right, but as part of characterisation and worldbuilding, delving into how belief interacts with, inspires or hinders an individual or a society. An example is in Roger Zelazny's Hugo Award-winning classic *Lord of Light* (1967), where colonists encounter the power of indigenous gods in a narrative device that moves the futuristic story forward.

In Ray Bradbury's short story "The Man" published in *The Illustrated Man* (2008), Captain Hart is a contemptuous man who seldom sleeps or eats, but drives himself in interspace travel from planet to planet in a rocket, in his faith quest. It's a science versus religion story, where Hart longs for something, for someone he cannot name—an inner quest that catapults him in pursuit for divine power. He arrives at Planet Forty-Three in Star System Three, and is infuriated to observe that the planet's inhabitants are indifferent to the rocket's arrival: how often do they get to see a spaceship? The reader swiftly understands what's behind the inhabitants' indifference and the peaceful nature of this world: the recent arrival of an itinerant messenger whose presence has placed them into a state of mysticism. But Hart refuses to believe, and falls into a murderous rage because no one is helping him to locate the real prophet of his quest. In a toxic religious quest, the captain jumps onto his rocket and shoots off to hunt down the very thing he has left behind. In this story, religion is not a plot point but rather a narrative device that simply moves the story forward.

The application of religion is more central as a plot point in dark fantasy and horror, like in the Netflix series *Midnight*

Mass (2021), or the movies *I Don't Want to Be Born* (1975) and *The Omen* (1976), where the interrogations of an omen are relative to a Roman Catholic protagonist's faith, and religion is the primary narrative driver, arriving its climax in ultimate combat with the angel of darkness. Such stories indulge our morbid infatuation with dark forces and Satan, and a story's enchantment warps us deeper in paradoxes that manifest evil in a child—an intrinsic vessel of innocence. Such horror stories generally adopt the trope 'religion will not save you', though sometimes it does. But what exactly is religion?

Religion means many things to many people.

The Vikings believed in Norse gods who bestowed meaning to the everyday, and invigorated warriors in battle, embracing dying to belong to Odin, the supreme god of the old religion. Vikings sacrificed to the gods to obtain favour (National Museum of Denmark, 2022), even to Loki—the crafty and deceitful god, up to no good but respected as the blood brother of Odin. Thor, the most popular deity, was the god of war and fertility who brought thunder and lightning in his chariot as he swung his hammer Mjöllnir.

The Aztecs had many gods, each representing an important aspect of the Aztec Empire and its history. These gods were integral to their beliefs and practices—contrary to the Spanish conquistadors who deemed the Aztecs pagan, in particular for their practice of human sacrifice atop a pyramid that entailed sculpting out a heart from a live victim. Other Aztec ritual sacrifices included death by starvation, death by flaying, death in battle or death by decapitation. Sometimes the sacrificed was a slave but, since death by sacrifice was an honour, sometimes it involved offspring or people of noble birth. Sacrifice appeased gods such as Tlaloc, who was 'of the earth', the giver of life, but whose wrath brought thunderstorms, floods, hail and lightning (History Crunch, 2022).

To believers of Buddhism, religion comprises meditation, spiritual and physical labour, and good behaviour to achieve enlightenment, or nirvana, away from the suffering of human life (National Geographic, 2022).

To African peoples—where Africa is not a single country—gods came along with creation myths woven into culture and belief systems. These gods were manifold, and mostly male, summoned by a diversity of traditional names:

> Among them are Mungu (Swahili in Tanzania), Imana (Banyarwanda in Rwanda), Wele (Abaluyia in Kenya), Rugaba (Ankore in Uganda), Juok (Anuak and Shilluk in the Upper Nile), Kanu (Baga in Guinea), Ngai (Gĩkũyũ in Kenya), Nzame (Bantu of the Congo), Ruwa (Chagga in Tanzania), and Umvelinqangi (Xhosa in South Africa) ('African Mythology'). Other gods, likely also male, include Avrikit (the fisherman god), Amun (god of air and sun), Magec (god of sun and light), Zivelele (the self-existent one), Wele (god of creation), and Bukulu (god of the sky) ('All'). There are female gods, too, such as Edinkira (Ashanti people in Ghana), the goddess of healing and blessing; Mwambwa (Lozi people in Namibia), the goddess of lust and desire; and Achimi (Kabyle people in Algeria), daughter of the buffalo god Itherther ('African Mythology'). All traditional gods, in particular those of creation, play an important role in African ideologies, identities, and origin stories. (Bacon, 2022, p.29–30)

Religion in African societies is not exclusive but rather enmeshed in the societal way of life, rendering itself a powerful tool to storytellers for worldbuilding, especially in tales that weave in magical realism. Nuzo Onoh—a British Nigerian author who fondly names herself the 'Queen of African Horror'—largely uses African spirituality to portray religion and drive the story forward in her fiction. Onoh's "Ogali" is a short story published in *Aurealis* #118, and is robust in its embrace of a marriage between religion and spirituality.

This short fiction "Ogali" casts a crucial gaze at black magic in subversive text set in rural Africa. Onoh draws attention to cultural mal/practice, social injustice and the plight of women in the Third World. A young girl has died. While she ailed on her deathbed, her clan despaired of the village priest and his desperate 'Hail Marys', and instead summoned a witchdoctor—more powerful than the priest's foreign Christian god—into Ogali's sick-room. The witchdoctor brewed and administered his pungent potions, sacred herbs and animal flesh to shield Ogali's soul from the nightly ghoul's evil eye to no avail. The witchdoctor now administers a ritual of soul-cleaning, using burial oils and charms, butchering cockerels and spraying the cursed compound with their blood to feed and ward off hovering ghosts. As villagers pay their last rites, the corpse, in this supernatural tale, seemingly points to the girl's killer by gripping the arm of a young man. The witchdoctor resumes his religious incantations to unveil this mystery.

Equally, in Onoh's *A Dance for the Dead* (2022), African spirituality carries the horror novel with the witchdoctor's crucial role in guiding the kingdom and appeasing the spirits:

> The oracle was speaking its message into the mind of their witchdoctor. The ancestral spirits of the Ngwu trees were naming the slave whose blood they would drink and whose heart would be devoured by the warriors, imbuing them with supernatural strength in the battleground. Again, Diké said a silent prayer for the protection of their house-slave, Ezekiel

Fat-Head, that his name be once again bypassed by the oracle on this occasion.
'Theresa Chicken-Legs! Theresa Chicken-Legs! Theresa Chicken-Legs!'
Three times the witch doctor shrieked the name of the chosen sacrifice as was directed by the oracle. (p.43)

David Coleman's approach to religion is dissimilar from Onoh's rendition in magical realism, but is closely aligned in its adoption of religion as an integral part of worldbuilding. Coleman's short story "The Shaming" ushers religion in a toxic utopia, where an organised belief system termed The Way (and it is Good) plants deep-rooted conviction in the story's protagonists, entrancing an entire society in fearful observance of rites and 'duty' and entrenching community spirituality into powerful personal belief that disregards bonds of kinship—shunning a person when they breach societal 'norms'.

"The Shaming" explores dichotomies between human nature and the mob in a world mastered by the Scrutineers. These governing peoples punish dissenters with a murderous shaming, a form of religious ritual that enacts away from the everyday living of the people. Ordinary folk cohabitate in poverty-stricken weatherboard shacks, their plod horses near collapse from severe labour, their ravenous pigs epitomising what will happen in The Shaming grounds, their chickens in muddy enclosures pecking at thin soil. The punishing ritual happens in what is termed The Proving Ground of The Shaming (the capitalisations idiosyncratic to the story), a dazzler stadium that is also a colosseum. The radiant amphitheatre is partitioned into bold colours aligned with where families must sit to observe and unwillingly partake in the punishments as they happen. The Way that is Good dictates everyday life in this totalitarian society. Indoctrinated folk are forever enshrouded in religious fear of falling out of favour and winding up in The Shaming grounds.

The Scrutineers question everything, even a girl's naming in a family comprising Blossom, Greener, Harvester, Vital:

> This name Rosie. You do know what a rose is. A worthless flower. Frivolous, ornamental, without redeeming characteristics. It cannot be eaten or used for any practical purpose. (p.39)

Rosie's uncle defends her, pulling all attention to himself:

> The child is named for all useful things. For the rosy dawn that takes us to our productive work. For the redness of our hands as we labour in all types of weather. For the glow of a forge as we form our tools. For the coloured clouds that tells us a Good day's work is done. (p.39)

What should be an 'ideal' society is in effect an invented world of mechanised order surrounding the Proper Way, where people and things are Good or Not Good.

Each observance of Good or Not Good in Coleman's story is a form of worship. Failure to adhere to its rules or principles culminates in a toxic and murderous rite in The Shaming grounds. There, society as a mass sacrifices its own for failing, through action or inaction, in their expression of faith, because Good is the Proper Way, the ideal albeit narrow charter that all must follow.

Religion as an Ideal

In a BBC guide on religious studies and belief, the Bitesize topic on God and truth states that—where Christianity is based on a single God represented by the Holy Trinity—the faith of many religions is centred on a god or gods. Religion introduced historical 'truth', as documented in the Christian Bible, moral 'truth', such as the commandments that determine right and wrong, absolute and religious 'truth' of the one true Almighty and whose truth comes in a sacred word or text (BBC Bitesize, 2023). In the examples discussed in this section, religious 'truth' comes from the spirits, gods or sacred text, sometimes through a human vessel such as an Aztec priest, a prophet, a chosen person, a wizard or a witchdoctor or, in "The Shaming", the Scrutineers with their doctrine of the 'Proper Way'.

Patrick Fagan (1996), on the Heritage Foundation, talks about why religion matters—it comes with enormous potential to address societal problems. Religion, in whichever form, encourages a people to believe in something, offering answers to quintessential questions on the meaning of life, and how a relationship with a higher being impacts upon that meaning (Greenstein, 2016). It can help a person find community and connection with other members, while at the same time heartening their sense of belonging and sentiments of mutuality in communal ritual and invigorating purpose. To an individual seeking something, whatever their quest, religion can be a pathway to redemption, hope, even peace. In the general moral compass that comes along with many religions, there are guidelines to live by (doing the right thing), teachings on respect, compassion, forgiveness and gratitude—as in Coleman's Way in "The Shaming".

Spirituality—also aligned with the Buddhist practice of meditation and finding enlightenment—bestows a sense of connection to something bigger than ourselves. It helps a person look within and without, nudging them to understand themselves and their fate after death, while also figuring out the greater answer of how they fit into the rest of the world they live in now. Religion helps people understand their interpretation of the meaning of life.

But religion can also be abused, leading to substantial spiritual abuse on individuals and whole communities.

Spiritual Abuse in Religion

Religion and colonialism

One prevalent example of religion and abuse is in the role of Christianity in the colonial expansion of western European powers. The Spanish conquistadors had no business bringing themselves to the world of the Aztecs other than empire building and a greed for Aztec gold—a quest mostly hidden in the guise of bringing religion to pagan peoples, who already had their own robust religious belief system.

In an article titled "The Reckoning of Religious Studies and Colonialism", Laura Ammon (2021) speaks to how the relationship between empire building and religious 'missionising' formed a legacy that continues to shape our world today, in a colonial matrix of power. The spread of Christianity throughout colonised worlds introduced its own cultural expectations of God's realm on earth, and the banishing of indigenous practices associated with tradition and culture. Christianity arrived under the excuse of discovery, introduced its own notion of 'good' and 'bad' in settler politics and modernity, and undermined entrenched systems of indigenous belief in occupied lands.

Many colonised people today are still healing, embracing decolonisation as a way of remembering, recognising and being as an integral thought change, challenging and resisting political practices and discourses sown by the coloniser (Nye, 2019, p.43). Resisters of decolonisation understand its threat to 'dominant forms of hegemony' within European, North American, Australasian and Pacific societies. Decolonisation encourages transfiguration from racial thinking, approaches and methodologies that marginalised indigenous people in their own lands.

Coleman's "The Shaming" offers a form of colonialism, where the dominant people are outsiders who live in tall-walled, stone buildings. The Scrutineers are lofty, rounded and well-fed, 'made of sharp angles, wind chapped cheek bones, pointing shoulders and jutting hips' (2018, online) compared to the humble townsfolk who are close to starvation in a world of plenty where collective exertion benefits only a few.

The Scrutineers make ordinary folk feel shame for their very existence. Their life is a perpetual atonement, as the Scrutineers use the 'Proper Way' to coerce them into giving more and more of themselves, to a point of psychological and emotional manipulation that leads largely harmless folk to inflict harm upon their very own.

Religion and persecutions

While early Christians experienced the brutality and violence of religious persecution in death by beating, sawing, flaying, stoning, beheading, crucifixion, boiling, burning at the stake, steaming alive inside a red-hot copper bull, the toxicity of religion introduced its own violence. The trials and persecution of 'witches'—who were sometimes victims of someone who wanted land or property, someone who disagreed with them, or someone whose advances they had rebuffed—are an example of this.

An infamous specimen of greed in land and property happened in 1307, where Jacques de Molay of the Templars suffered the wrath of King Philip IV of France—deeply in debt to the Templars. The king persecuted the Templars, enabling their torture into making false confessions on charges including sodomy. Upon retracting his statements, likely made under torment, de Molay was burned as a relapsed heretic by Philip's officers the same afternoon (Britannica, 2022).

In another example, a *Guardian* news story reported that Massachusetts lawmakers had formally exonerated Elizabeth Johnson Jr, who was sentenced to death in 1693 at the height of the Salem witch trials:

> Twenty people from Salem and neighbouring towns were killed and hundreds of others accused during a frenzy of Puritan injustice that began in 1692, stoked by superstition, fear of disease and strangers, scapegoating and petty jealousies. Nineteen were hanged, and one man was crushed to death by rocks. (Yang, 2022)

Individuals and communities use religion to control spouses, to justify violence, to make money, to control the masses, to discriminate, to manipulate, or to make personal gain. Signs of spiritual abuse include an attempt to exert power and control over someone using religion, faith or belief (WebMD, 2022).

Religious abuse in both of Nuzo Onoh's stories emerges in the hands of the very witchdoctor in which the society places its trust. In "Ogali", it turns out that the witchdoctor encouraged the young man's father, Obioha—stricken with AIDS—to rape a virgin in order to pass on his 'curse', and find himself cured—which, of course, is a fallacy.

In *A Dance for the Dead*, the witchdoctor uses the pretext of engaging with the spirit world and ventriloquism through an oracle to douse revenge: vindictive harm on the sacrificial girl, Theresa Chicken-Legs, who rebuffed his advances; an evil eye on anyone who defended her—even the king's own heir—by cursing them to societal ostracisation.

The Scrutineers in "The Shaming" carry out religious abuse by introducing class and forced labour, encouraging mob mentality where the collective becomes a subconscious harming, using the everyday people's own supernatural power of touch against their own. It takes courage in the young girl, Rosie, to make a stand against the Scrutineers—she swerves her touch to save her dissenting uncle, easy-natured and critical of tyranny, condemned to die in The Shaming grounds.

Toxic religion in these stories manifests itself in abuse to the faithful from incumbents in power who use fear, intimidation, violence, even psychological harms to control, humiliate, pressure others, or obligate them to act against their wills, with serious consequences for adults and children. In Coleman's "The Shaming", it takes a child's courage to save her uncle and subsequently her people:

> The three Bull Husks were directed by the intense Touch focus of hundreds upon hundreds... Bent on the will of the Overseer, the Authority.
> 'I can't just sit here and watch this...' Rosie sobbed... She watched aghast as Uncle Vital dutifully sat up, dutifully exposing his torso to the blades, improving the spectacle...
> Rosie exploded from her seat, screaming from the very bottom of her soul. She felt something break in her mind, a great dam of energy welling and transcending every part of her essence. An outpouring of golden light expanded her Touch a thousand-fold, a thousand times more, an inferno

enough to consume her completely. The energy bellowed for
release, and she let it go with the force of hurricanes.
'You will stop that now,' she commanded, her voice deep and
resonant. 'Each. Bull. Stop.' (p.51)

A similar transformation arc manifests itself in Onoh's "Ogali" where the villagers finally understand the wrong that has happened. Though the witchdoctor escapes their wrath, the rapist doesn't:

Even before he finished speaking, the crowd descended on
Obioha of Okoro clan, led by Ogali's grieving father. They
tore into him, limb by limb, using their fists, their feet, sticks,
stones and every sharp implement they could find to end his
accursed life.
It was a mad orgy of blind violence and the witchdoctor
could only stare in fatalistic resignation as Obioha bled into
the soil in a blood sacrifice of atonement. (p.23)

In *A Dance for the Dead*, maggot-infested corpses in shades of reek and grave-soil lurch to mete justice on the once-sacred man, Dibia Okpoko. He must perform one more cleansing rite before yielding to the claws of the undead, whose innocence he had snatched in life.

In "The Shaming", Rosie's action and consequence offer their own transformation arc in a story that shows how sometimes justice prevails and discloses toxic religion to those who suffer it, those who must find courage to resist it—to the astoundment of the perpetrators.

The three primary works that this essay explores demonstrate the use and misuse of religion in utopian and cultural societies, and a semblance of redemption to undo wrong. When employed in fiction, including speculative fiction, religion offers authors a wealth of thematic plots and subplots to imbue characterisation, layer worldbuilding, and apply the psychoanalytical gaze at the motivations of individuals or a collective towards an objective that may be integral to the story's transformation arc.

As Nuzo Onoh says tongue-in-cheek in an epithet of an African idiom at the start of her novel:

> 'When a man's penis grows too big for his loincloth, he shouldn't be shocked when a monkey mistakes it for its banana.'

References

Ammon, L., 2021. The Reckoning of Religious Studies and Colonialism. *Canopy Forum: On the Interactions of Law & Religion.* [online] Available at: <https://canopyforum.org/2021/03/19/the-reckoning-of-religious-studies-and-colonialism/> [Accessed 4 June 2022].

Bacon, E., 2022. *An Earnest Blackness*. Ohio: Anti-Oedipus Press.

BBC Bitesize, 2023. God and Truth. [online] Available at < https://www.bbc.co.uk/bitesize/guides/zv2fgwx/revision/1> [Accessed 4 April 2023].

Bradbury, R., 2008. *The Illustrated Man*. London: Harper Collins.

Britannica 2022. Jacques de Molay. [online] Available at <https://www.britannica.com/biography/Jacques-de-Molay> [Accessed 4 June 2022].

Coleman, D., 2018. "The Shaming". *Dimension6*: Issue 15 (October 2018). [online] Available at: https://coeurdelion.com.au/dimension6 [Accessed 4 June 2022].

Fagan, P., 1996. Why Religion Matters: The Impact of Religious Practice on Social Stability. [online] Available at <https://www.heritage.org/civil-society/report/why-religion-matters-the-impact-religious-practice-social-stability> [Accessed 4 June 2022].

Greenstein, L., 2016. The Mental Health Benefits of Religion & Spirituality. [online] Available at <https://www.nami.org/Blogs/NAMI-Blog/December-2016/The-Mental-Health-Benefits-of-Religion-Spiritual> [Accessed 4 June 2022].

History Crunch 2022. Aztec Religion. [online] Available at <https://www.historycrunch.com/aztec-religion.html#/> [Accessed 4 June 2022].

IMDB 2022. *I Don't Want to Be Born*. [online]. Available at <https://www.imdb.com/title/tt0072867> [Accessed 2 October 2022].

IMDB 2022. *Midnight Mass*. [online]. Available at <https://www.imdb.com/title/tt10574558> [Accessed 2 October 2022].

IMDB 2022. *The Omen*. [online]. Available at < https://www.imdb.com/title/tt0075005> [Accessed 2 October 2022].

National Geographic 2022. Buddhism. [online] Available at < https://education.nationalgeographic.org/resource/buddhism> [Accessed 4 June 2022].

National Museum of Denmark 2022. Religion, Magic, Death and Rituals. [online] Available at < https://en.natmus.dk/historical-knowledge/denmark/prehistoric-period-until-1050-ad/the-viking-age/religion-magic-death-and-rituals/> [Accessed 4 June 2022].

Nye, M., 2019. Decolonizing the Study of Religion. *Open Library of Humanities*, 5(1), p.43. [online] Available at <http://doi.org/10.16995/olh.421> [Accessed 4 June 2022].

Onoh, N., 2022. *A Dance for the Dead*. Texas: Stygian Median Sky.

Onoh, N. "Ogali". *Aurealis* #118 (March 2018): p.13–24.

Yang, M. 2022. Last Salem 'Witch' Pardoned 329 Years After She Was Wrongly Convicted. *The Guardian*. [online] Available at < https://www.theguardian.com/us-news/2022/may/27/last-salem-witch-pardoned-elizabeth-johnson-jr-massachusetts> [Accessed 4 June 2022].

Zelazny, R. 1967. *Lord of Light*. New York: Doubleday.

An Agnostic's Prayer. The Egyptian gods in speculative fiction and Roger Zelazny

Steph P Bianchini

Abstract

There are few speculative fiction writers in which religion in all its forms and traditions has played a role as important as in the work of Roger Zelazny. From the Chinese characters in *Lord Demon* to the Siddhartha-type god of *Lord of Light*, the incredible richness of the world's spirituality is portrayed in his work in an astonishing depth. But it is probably in *Creatures of Light and Darkness* that Zelazny reaches the most original and poignant treatment of mythology. In a narrative voice that mixes prose and poems, the Egyptian gods come alive in a weird and fascinating far-future setting, making us wonder what the meaning of being a god is and which kind of gods we consider as such. That question drives the novel, as well as this article.

1. Introduction

If Science Fiction (SF) is full of aliens, Roger Zelazny was maybe one of them.

After all, the originality of his novels was impressive, both in terms of cultural content and experimental format, as a quick look at his fiction demonstrates.

One of the subjects where this originality is most evident is religion. In Zelazny's work, gods from across the world come alive like protagonists or antagonists and are more than just literary devices to make the action move (like Euripidian *deux ex machina*). Many of his novels feature divinities of some kind, both historical and completely fictional.

Lord Demon and *Lord of Light*—this one considered by many Zelazny's masterpiece—engage with Chinese and Indian spirituality, featuring Taoist gods and bodhisattva types, while the spotlight of *Creatures of Light and Darkness*[1], as far as religion is concerned, is on the Egyptian Gods, or better said, Zelazny's take on them.

A disclaimer. A lot has been written on this unique novel from a literary perspective, due to its mixed prose-poetry format—after all, it started as an experiment—and the difficulties of categorising it in a specific genre (some consensus is about fantasy with strong science-fiction and cyberpunk influences and elements of horror). After all, *Creatures of Light and Darkness* was published after Zelazny's friend, fellow author Samuel R. Delany, encouraged him to do so. The book is dedicated to Delany, to whom it probably owes its existence.

Creatures of Light and Darkness received its fair share of criticism, too, in terms of lack of character development and some logical issues in the plot—briefly discussed in the next section.

This article does not discuss any of it, because the focus here is on the Egyptian gods it portrays and the way the writer manages to make them both historically recognisable and originally conceived. This is not the first or the only time

---

1. Not a lot has been written about the impact of Egyptian mythology in speculative fiction, or fiction whatsoever. However, recently some interest has been recorded, as a conference organised by the University of Birmingham on 9-10 July 2021, "Do Ancient Egyptians Dream of Electric Sheep? The Reception of the Ancient Egyptian in Science Fiction" (an obvious reference to PKD's piece that inspired *Blade Runner*) proves.

Ancient Egypt's pantheon appears in fiction, but certainly one of the most prominent, and well worth an in-depth analysis.

2. The novel

The best summary of *Creatures of Light and Darkness* is probably the existing print edition featuring the Lord of the House of Dead, Anubis, on its cover.

> Two gods, two houses, one quest, and the eternal war between life and death. To save his kingdom, Anubis, Lord of the Dead, sends forth his servant on a mission of vengeance. At the same time, from The House of Life, Osiris sends forth his son, Horus, on the same mission to destroy utterly and forever The Prince Who Was a Thousand. But neither of these superhuman warriors is prepared for the strange and harrowing world of mortal life, and The Thing That Cries in the Night may well destroy not only their worlds, but all mankind. (Zelazny, 1969, cover)

The main elements of the novel are all there.

It is a war to save humanity from an unknown but terrifying force.

It is a revenge story (of Anubis and Osiris against the Prince Who Was a Thousand).

But it is also a quest within a quest. Anubis's servant Wakim is tasked to find and destroy the Prince Who Was a Thousand (first quest). He also carries as a name that is not his own, and the discovery of his true name (he is the God Set the Destroyer) will alter the course of the war itself. And it is much more than that.

One of the criticisms about this novel is that it requires more than one reading for a deep understanding, as it is set in the far future—i.e, in a landscape not familiar for the reader—sprawled across many worlds with exotic names mixing Egyptian mythology, original fiction and time warps at times difficult to follow.

The plot can also at times become a bit confusing, because we are told the identity of some of the main characters (Wakim-Set) only later in the book, together with a complicated backstory—divergent from the original Egyptian mythology—and even more complex evolution of the novel's action.

As far as the backstory goes, everything was once ruled by Thoth (first introduced as The Prince Who Was a Thousand, whose identity is revealed only in media res) with his Angels (other gods not necessarily named) divided in "Stations" or "Houses"[2]. They confront something called the Nameless, or the Thing That Cries in The Night, a dark and mortal force that can destroy the universe, without success. Chaos unravels, with Stations becoming vacated, Angels scattering around taking over deserted places, and the threat still looming ahead. Osiris and Anubis are the only two Angels actually at work when the novel starts. Osiris is the Lord of the House of Life, which Anubis, the Master of the House of the Dead, works to destroy.

Back to the present action in the novel, where Set, introduced as Wakim, is sent by Anubis to find and kill Thoth (to whom he is related, although he cannot remember it) and so does Osiris, who sends instead his son Horus for it.

What happens next is both entertaining and surprising, especially for what concerns the main characters, who are,

---

2. These Stations seem to be many, but only a few are named, and when it happens it is because one character is related to them. The House of the Dead (Anubis), the House of Life (Osiris), the House of Fire (Typhon) etc.

with few exceptions (Madrak, Vramin) all gods. However, what matters the most is which kind of gods we are looking at.

3. The character-gods

One of the main points often observed about the novel is that *Creatures of Light and Darkness* is first and foremost science fiction and fantasy, and it is not based on actual ancient Egyptian mythology. According to this thesis, the characters and events in the novel, such as Anubis, Osiris, Horus, and Isis, are fictional creations that only share the names and minor details of the original Egyptian pantheon, but no more than that.

While there's some truth in that—after all, there are also some obvious differences on the Egyptian gods as portrayed in the novel and their historical counterparts in mythology[3], which will be shown later in this section—I tend to disagree overall.

This is because the portrayal is far more accurate than it looks like at a first reading, and it can be understood only by an in-depth comparison with not only the mythology, but also the evolution of the centuries of those myths, which have been altering quite substantially the characteristic of the gods themselves[4].

---

3. Just to make an example among many, in the ancient Egyptian mythology, Thoth was not the top god or the ruler of the universe, and he was not associated with the Houses of Life and Death.

4. The complexity of the Egyptian pantheon cannot be underestimated, especially when one tries to follow its adaptation in fiction and dealing with its evolutions over time. *"The Egyptians had no problem with a multitude of gods and they seldom shelved old deities in favour of new ones. Characteristics and roles of various gods were syncretized to reconcile differing religious beliefs, customs, or ideals. For political and religious reasons, for example, the Theban god Amun, who was considered the most*

This starts with the iconography but also with their attributions and appellatives, and a comparison with the Egyptian originals. Here we are going to discuss in detail only the most important ones.

3.1. The Jackal-headed Anubis, Ruler of the "House of Dead"

Anubis is the god the reader meets just at the beginning of the novel[5], which starts with a gathering in the House of the Dead where Anubis reigns.

Anubis is a well-known feature of the Egyptian pantheon, and one of the main criticisms of the novel is that his attributions in the original mythology are not the same of this role in the novel. The myths, the critics claim, say that Anubis is a psychopomp—of the kind of the Greek Hermes—someone who accompanies the souls in their underworld journey. He is associated with the dead, but he is not the God of the Afterlife, whose attribution belongs instead to Osiris, at least in the most modern tradition.

Which is only partially true, as a matter of fact[6].

What is certain is that, in the novel, in addition to be the God

---

powerful deity in the New Kingdom, was united with Ra, a sun god whose cult dated to the beginnings of Egypt. Worship of the gods of Egypt evolved over time as large cults developed on a local and then on a national scale," (Bunson, 1991, p.99).

5. It is not surprising that the novel starts with Anubis. After all, the Jackal god is *the* Egyptian god in modern pop culture, the one most immediately recognisable and most popular. See TV Tropes (2023) for a good analysis of Anubis's fortune as the Ancient Egyptian symbol.

6. This is due to the complexity and the longevity of Egyptian Mythology, which was regionally connected, with cities having their own gods in different periods in time. As a consequence, much as it happened with the Greek mythology, the myths often were mixed up and gods deconstructed and reassembled to give origin to new myths and news gods. Anubis's example is quite a telling one.

of the Afterlife, he is a dog-faced god who enjoys watching the souls playing games and having fun and, in general, looks more shallow than the mythology would suggest.

However, at a certain moment in the long Egyptian history, Anubis was the god of the dead as it is in the moment. In the actual Egyptian pantheon, Anubis plays a very important role and goes through a long evolution over the many centuries of Egyptian civilisation, to the point that there exists more than one myth of his origin. In one, probably older than the other, he is the son of Ammon-Ra (the Sun god) and Hesat, and associated with the mummification process[7] and the underworld in general. It is at these early times that Anubis is revered as the god of the dead.

Things change during the Middle Kingdom, that long period of power consolidation that goes from the end of the Eleventh Dynasty to the Thirteenth Dynasty, roughly between 21 BCE to 17 BCE. This is the moment of Osiris's ascent as the most powerful deity in the Egyptian pantheon—see below for the Osiris myth.

From this moment onward, Anubis's origins are rewritten, and he becomes associated with Osiris, becoming his and Nephtys's son. Some of his attributes—and denominations—shift to Osiris and Anubis loses his status of 'Lord of the Dead' although not his importance in the Egyptian pantheon.

One important source for Anubis's attribution is *The Book of the Dead*, where he holds a scale and measures a man's heart against the truth and decides if the deceased deserves to enter the realm of the dead. Anubis is the God of writing and guardian of the Universe Thoth, which in Zelazny's novel

---

[7]. This association remained even when later on Anubis became linked to Osiris. In the Osiris myth, it is Anubis who helps Isis to embalm Osiris's martyrised body.

plays the role of the Prince Who Was a Thousand and the villain Anubis wants Wakim/Set to kill (things will of course go differently).

Anubis's popularity continued even in the Greek and Roman times, where he becomes associated with other gods linked to the underworld, such as Hermes—whose original function he fulfilled—but also to the three-headed Cerberus and even Hades/Pluto, the Roman god of the dead.

FIGURE 1—(from left) Osiris, Anubis, Horus in ancient Egypt's imagery[8]

---

8. One thing that remains common in both the myth and the novel is the colour associated with the gods. Osiris has hues of green, the way he has in the official iconography because, of course, he is a corpse. Anubis is black, the result of the discolouration of the corpse after its treatment for the embalmment. However, for the Ancient Egyptians, the colour black was also associated with fertility and therefore rebirth in the afterlife, due to the colour of the fertile silt of the Nile river.
(Source: By derivative work: A. Parrot (talk) La_tombe_de_Horemheb_

An interesting comparison between the existing iconography (Figure 1) and one that could be drawn by applying the description from the novel is presented in this extract:

> Anubis lowers his black muzzle slightly and his fangs are white within it. Red lightning, his tongue, darts forward, re-enters his mouth. He stands then, and the shadows slide downward upon his man-formed body. (1969, p.4)

3.2. The bird-headed Orisis, ruler of the "House of Life"

The same complex mix between fiction and real mythology attributions we noticed with Anubis can be said for the Ruler of the House of Life, Osiris, as well. However, in this case there are even more intriguing melanges and deviations from the tradition between the novel's characters and the mythology, starting from the family ties.

As in the Egyptian pantheon, Osiris is married with Isis and has a son called Horus.

The novel doesn't say much, however, of the backstory regarding Isis, Osiris's sister and wife, and even less of their present relationship apart from the fact she's called 'the Red Witch' and she's portrayed as constantly dreaming[9].

(KV.57)_(Vallée_des_Rois_Thèbes_ouest)-4.jpg: Jean-Pierre Dalbéra - La_tombe_de_Horemheb_(KV.57)_(Vallée_des_Rois_Thèbes_ouest)_-4.jpg, CC BY 2.0, https://commons.wikimedia.org/w/index.php?curid=5611130)

9. From the novel, we do not get the perception of how powerful and important Isis was in the Egyptian pantheon and, in general, for the whole of Mediterranean culture. Her popularity and longevity is comparable only to Anubis, and so are her later incarnations in different cultures. "*After the conquest of Egypt by Alexander the Great in 331 BCE, her worship traveled to Greece and then to Rome. During the time of the Roman Empire, she was worshipped in every corner of their realm from Britain through Europe to Anatolia. The Cult of Isis was the strongest opponent of the new religion of Christianity between the 4th-6th centuries CE, and iconography, as well*

The most apparent divergent attribution from fact/fiction is the fact that Osiris is associated with the House of Life, while he was, at least from the Middle Kingdom onward, the powerful God of the Dead. Zelazny portrays Osiris and Anubis fighting against each other for life and death in the worlds—nothing resembling a conflict between the two deities is recorded in the original texts.

However, even this is less puzzling than it looks. Osiris is, after all, the God of the harvest, of resurrection and rebirth, all attributes of life. He becomes the Lord of the Dead only because he dies and decides to remain in the Underworld.

And regarding his character, earlier myths portray him in a less benevolent form[10].

In terms of the iconography, Osiris is farther away from the mythological Osiris even in the way he's described from a beholder.

> Looking up, he sees the orange, green, yellow and black bird-head of Osiris. (1969, p.48)

Now compare the Anubis and Osiris of the novel with the actual mythology, starting with the way they look.

What we immediately notice when looking at Figure 3—a fresco coming from archaeological findings—is that these three character-gods are as strongly linked in the actual mythology as they are in the novel. The difference is that

---

as tenets of belief, of the Isis cult were incorporated into the new faith. Imagery of the Virgin Mary holding her son Jesus comes directly from Isis cradling her son Horus and the Dying and Reviving God figure of Jesus himself is a version of Osiris," (Mark, 2016:7).

10. It is only when his popularity grows that Osiris becomes 'the good one', unfairly killed by his villainous brother Set. Incidentally, Osiris dies more than once in the Egyptian myths, and even in Zelazny's novel he ends up dying in action.

Zelazny mixes them up in terms of names, attributes and even iconography. The one in the novel who is portrayed with a bird face is Osiris, while in the original pantheon Osiris looks completely human.

It is Horus[11], his son, who has a bird face—in the pantheon, but not in the novel.

This mixing up of this triad is also observable in the other gods—i.e., the ones who are not immediately introduced with their name and whose name is found out during the novel. The most important is of course the champion of the House of the Dead, Wakim, who turns out to be no other than Set. Like Set, he shares a few characteristics with Osiris, some actually existing in real mythology and others that do not or that belong to other gods[12].

---

11. Compared to the role he has in the Egyptian pantheon, Horus's role in the novel is limited to the point that there is not a lot in terms of attribution and agency, apart from the fact that he is tasked with the elimination of Thoth by his father Osiris. But we would be mistaken by thinking him a minor god. Far from it. "*An early avian god who became one of the most important deities in ancient Egypt. Associated with the sun, sky, and power, Horus became linked with the king of Egypt as early as the First Dynasty (c. 3150-2890 BCE). Although the name 'Horus' might refer to a number of avian deities it principally designates two: Horus the Elder, one of the first five gods born at the beginning of creation, and Horus the Younger who was the son of Osiris and Isis. Following the rise in popularity of the Osiris Myth, Horus the Younger became one of the most important gods in Egypt. In the story, after Osiris is murdered by his brother Set, Horus is raised by his mother in the Delta swamps. When he comes of age, he battles his uncle for the kingdom and wins, restoring order to the land. The kings of Egypt, with some exceptions, all linked themselves with Horus in life and with Osiris in death. The king was thought to be the living incarnation of Horus and, through him, the god gave all good things to his people. He is usually depicted as a man with the head of a hawk but is represented by many different images,*" (Mark, 2016:6). Horus is probably where the novel detaches itself the most from the original myths.

12. For instance, Set/Wakim's own dismembering mirrors Osiris's backstory in the Osiris myths. However, Set's banishment to the desert

His antagonistic relationship with Horus is true in the novel as much as in the original myths[13].

The above analysis demonstrates that the linkage between the mythology and the novel is stronger than it may appear at first glance, although Zelazny's genius deconstructs and recombines them in an original and powerful melange, not for this less authentic.

The attention to mythological detail can also be seen in the onomastic, which can be traced back to the ancient mythology (Egyptian and otherwise), and it is the way the characters are named by definitions and attributions.

Although there are not (always) the same[14] as exists in Egyptian mythology, they are perfectly plausible because they were structured in the same way of the original ones.

Anubis had, for instance, many of them in the actual pantheon.

Among the most notable:

---

lands after he loses his battle with Horus reminds us of the start of the novel, where Set has spent one thousand years in the House of Dead being Anubis's apprentice.

13. In the actual original Egyptian pantheon, the Horus myths are actually responsible for turning an overall powerful but benevolent god—Set—into a villain. This fact illustrates one of the salient points of Egyptian mythology. "*Many gods and goddesses, such as Set or Serket, transformed through time to take on other roles and responsibilities. These transformations were sometimes dramatic, as in the case of Set who went from a hero protector-god to a villain and the world's first murderer. Serket was almost certainly an early Mother Goddess, and her later role as protector against venomous creatures (especially scorpions) and guardian of women and children reflects those characteristics,*" (Mark, 2016:1).

Creatures of Light and Darkness offers a more positive view of Set, which is, again, not entirely made up but representing something already existing in the actual myths.

14. Interestingly, Set is called 'The Destroyer', both in the novel and in the original myth, associated as he was with war.

- "First of the Westerners" (for the association with the underworld, ie, the sunset, and therefore the West direction. More recently in the Egyptian history, this became the way Osiris was addressed);
- "Ruler of the Nine Bows" (direct reference to the nine traditional enemies of the realm);
- "The Dog Who Swallows Millions" (because he is the god of death and swallows souls);
- "Master of Secrets" (because he is the one aware of what awaits after death);
- "Lord of the Sacred Land" (where the sacred land is the desert where necropolis are located).

All the same, they serve both as a literary device and return a feeling of authenticity of this fictional, divine world.

4. The nature of the (Egyptian) gods

The second point to discuss here, and a more philosophical one, is the way the gods behave in the novel and the way the divine worldbuilding, so to speak, is set.

If for God we intend a perfect being with supreme power who created the cosmos, the characters in the book do not qualify[15]. However, if we take the definition of God from deities of Eastern or even Greek cultures, we find they are anthropomorphic entities who have a human (or half-beast, half-human) body but are endowed with supernatural capabilities and, to a certain extent, immortality.

Of course, there was nothing in the original Egyptian pantheon like Zelazny's Station-holding gods, let alone gods

---
15. Although the Nameless in the book could. See below in the text for what he represents.

waging war against each other to save the universe from a threat. And while, as we have seen, there were certainly associations of some of them with the world of the dead, or others that were assigned certain areas of competency, the depiction of gods holding stations in the universe is original to Zelazny.

Which is not to say that it is completely abstracted from the mythology tradition as a whole. Actually, there is a nearby pantheon that is a closer match to the world as described in *Creatures of Light and Darkness*: The Olympian gods.

Together with some clear references to the Judaic traditions—the Angels, and especially the Nameless[16], the Older God who must be destroyed but cannot— Greek mythology is the other that informs the most Zelazny's worldbuilding, a truly fascinating syncretism which is one of the most intriguing aspects of this novel.

When the novel speaks about the Houses (sometimes called Stations), it reminds us of the Olympic gods and the link they had with the world of humanity.

This is because, as the historians of religion showed in many studies[17], all the Greek cities used to track their descent to one or more gods, and that was the cultural basis of the concept of "genos".

The genos is what establishes people sharing the same lineage, and the Greek polis is a city destined to welcome people who have the same origin[18]; that is, who belong to the

---

16. The reference here to Yahweh is clear, together with the impossibility of naming the god.

17. Dario Sabbatucci among them, writing many books on the relationship between myths, rites, history, and genos.

18. This belonging is more important than any law of the city, and nothing shows this better than the Greek tragedy *Antigone*, by Sophocles, where there are two opposing principles in conflict. Antigone is torn between the

same "House", which each God claims as their own.

As such, Athena is the Protector of the city of Athens, while the God looking after Sparta's Station (to use Zelazny's term) is Apollo. Stations could be also swapped—such as Thebes in different times of its existence—and gods can be the Protectors of more than one city.

Moreover, the behaviour of Zelazny's gods is closer to the ones observed in the cycles of Olympian (and pre-Olympian) Greek gods, in their cosmic conflicts and endless bickering and revenge plots, and especially constant interfering with the human world than the distant deities of the Egyptian pantheon.

So, yes, *Creatures of Light and Darkness* are gods in their own right, and they behave as such.

5. After Creatures of Light and Darkness: Echoes of Egyptian mythology.

No other work of speculative fiction portrayed the Egyptian gods in such detail and beauty, artistic freedom notwithstanding. It does not mean it is the only one.

The ancient Egyptians have proved to be captivating, and their influence has been widespread in speculative fiction across various media, from Roland Emmerich's *Stargate* to *Star Trek*, passing through Enki Bilal's *Immortal*, to Luc Besson's *The Extraordinary Adventures of Adele Blanc Sec* and even *The Fifth Element*, videogames such as *Tomb Raider* (whose final chapter, *The Last Revelation*, is completely set in Egypt) and *Dawn of War*, and manga like *Ghost in the Shell*.

Another good example are Japanese anime, where themes and references to the Egyptian pantheon are widespread,

---

will to bury her brother who fell in combat even if for the law he became an enemy of the city. Law against genos.

featuring, for instance, the *Dragon Ball* franchise, and in characters from *Kamigami No Asobi*, *Jo Jo's Bizarre Adventure*, *Kamigami No Ki*, *Oh, Suddenly Egyptian Gods*. And, of course, the franchise *Yu-Gi-Oh!*.

Yu-Gi-Oh! whose original manga by Kazuki Takahashi began publication back in 1996, is probably the most accomplished example of the integration of complex Egyptian myths into Japanese pop culture. The manga follows Yugi Mutou, who solves a mystery coming from Ancient Egypt called the Millennium Puzzle, which grants Yugi an alter-ego gambler and catapults him into all sort of adventures. There are Egyptian gods[19] in there, and, of course, Anubis features prominently among them[20].

Even when not playing as main characters in full novels—like, say, Tim Powers' book The Anubis Gates (1983)—cultural echoes and references to Egyptian gods kept popping up in speculative fiction.

A recent but telling example is Red Rising, the first instalment of a world-famous series by Pierce Brown. While built on completely different premises—Red Rising is a solid work of science fiction with dystopian qualities, while Creatures of Light and Darkness is mainly fantasy with some cyberpunk/science fiction elements—there are a lot of references (intentional or not) in the second to the structure of the Institute, the Gold's elite high school for future leaders. It

---

19. Or references to them. Yugi's rival in gaming in the series, for instance, is called Seto Kaiba, a direct reference to the god Set.

20. Anubis is one of the protagonists of *Yu-Gi-Oh! Duel Monsters: Pyramid of Light*, the first film based on the anime rendition of the franchise. In there, Anubis's tomb is uncovered by archaeologists, complete with his most precious artefact, the Pyramid of Light. Yugi Mutou manages to awaken Anubis's spirit, who, in the movie, is a malevolent presence, closer to Zelazny's depiction of a capricious Anubis than to the real Anubis of the myths.

is divided into Houses, each one with a territory, tokens, and a proctor with a Greek's god name, in competition against each other for supremacy. One of the main characters—Darrow's brilliant and infamous antagonist, the only one who can really match him in the series—Adrius au Augustus—belongs to the House Pluto.

The association with the Underworld can't be made more evident by the fact their members call themselves Boneriders and the most faithful minion of Adrius is Lilath (the name matches closely the Biblical Lilith, a she-demon and Adam's first wife). Therefore, how else can Adrius be nicknamed in the novel?

The Jackal, of course—courtesy of Anubis.

6. Conclusions

If Zelazny himself has a peculiar place in the speculative fiction world as a gifted portrayer of the world's spirituality transfused into narrative, *Creatures of Light and Darkness* is a quite original piece among works of consistently high standards.

After all, it features what is probably the most famous prayer in a speculative fiction novel:

> Insofar as I may be heard by anything, which may or may not care what I say, I ask, if it matters, that you be forgiven for anything you may have done or failed to do which requires forgiveness. Conversely, if not forgiveness but something else may be required to ensure any possible benefit for which you may be eligible after the destruction of your body, I ask that this, whatever it may be, be granted or withheld, as the case may be, in such a manner as to insure your receiving said benefit. I ask this in my capacity as your elected intermediary

between yourself and that which may not be yourself, but which may have an interest in the matter of your receiving as much as it is possible for you to receive of this thing, and which may in some way be influenced by this ceremony. Amen. (1969, pp.32-33)

However, what makes the novel such as a unique piece is the syncretic representation of one of the most fascinating pantheons ever created by humanity, the Egyptian gods.

As of today, nobody in the speculative fiction world has been able to match Zelazny's mastery.

Bibliography

Armour, R., 1986. *Gods and Myths of Ancient Egypt*. Cairo: The American University in Cairo Press

Brown P., 2014. *Red Rising*. NYC: Del Rey Books.

Bunson, M., 2014. *Encyclopedia of ancient Egypt*. NYC: Infobase Publishing.

Mark, J.J., 2016. Egyptian Gods: The Complete List. World History Encyclopedia. [online] Available at: <https://www.worldhistory.org/article/885/egyptian-gods---the-complete-list/> [Accessed 23-12-2022].

Power. T., 1983. *The Anubis Gates*. London: ACE.

Sabbatucci, D., 1978. *Il mito, il rito e la storia*. Roma: Bulzoni.
---, 1984. *Da Osiride a Quirino: corso di Storia delle Religioni 1983-1984*. Roma: Il Bagatto.

Shaw, G.J., 2014. *The Egyptian Myths: A Guide to the Ancient Gods and Legends*. London: Thames & Hudson.

Sophocles, Antigone. [online] Available at: <https://ir.canterbury.ac.nz/handle/10092/9681> [Accessed 23-12-2022].

TV Tropes. 2023. The Egyptian mythology. [online] Available at: <https://tvtropes.org/pmwiki/pmwiki.php/Characters/EgyptianMythology> [Accessed 23-12-2022].

University of Birmingham. 2021. *Do Ancient Egyptians Dream of Electric Sheep? The Reception of Ancient Egyptian in Science Fiction*, conference organised on 9-10 July 2021. Birmingham, UK. Programme available at: <https://www.birmingham.ac.uk/schools/historycultures/departments/caha/events/2021/do-ancient-egyptians-dream-of-electric-sheep.aspx> [Accessed 23-12-2022].

Zelazny, R., 1968. *Lord of light*. NYC: Avon Books.
---, 1969. *Creatures of Light and Darkness*. NYC: Avon Books.

Zelazny, R. & J. Lindskold, 1999. *Lord Demon*. NYC: Avon Books.

LIST OF MANGA AND ANIME CITED

Dragon Ball
Kamigami No Asobi
Jo Jo's Bizarre Adventure
Kamigami No Ki
Oh, Suddenly Egyptian Gods
Yu-Gi-Oh!
Saint-Seiya

Darling, You're Just Divine!
Queer Gods in science fiction and fantasy

Cheryl Morgan

Abstract

In modern Western society, we tend to assume that religion is the enemy of the LGBTQ+ community. Some religious people certainly give us plenty of ground for thinking that. Outside the Abrahamic religions, however, attitudes towards queer people could be very different. Some gods were decidedly queer. Also the history of the Abrahamic religions is nowhere near as heteronormative and cisnormative as some modern church leaders would like to make out.

This paper will look at queer gods from history and their provenances. It will look at how the gender of god/s is understood. It will also argue that for much of human history, religious cults were one of the main safe spaces for queer people.

*

'The power to turn a man into a woman, and a woman into a man, is yours, Inanna!'

This is part of a hymn to the goddess Inanna, attributed to the Sumerian princess and high priestess, Enheduanna, who lived in the 23rd century BCE (Enheduanna). We cannot know exactly what she meant by those words. Possibly she was just playing with gender stereotypes and meant that Inanna made men afraid and women brave. Maybe she meant that the goddess caused people to be attracted to people of their own sex. Maybe she was talking about social, or even medical, gender transition. Whatever the true explanation, however, there is no doubt that the cult of Inanna, or Ishtar as she became known in Babylon and Assyria, had a lot of involvement in gender and sexual ambiguity. This will be explained in greater detail later in this paper, but the story of queer religion begins long before the start of recorded history.

The idea that divinity and gender ambiguity are related is commonplace in tribal cultures around the world. The Greek historian Herodotus reports that among the Scythians there was a group of shamanic people known as Enarees (Herodotus). These were people who had been assigned male at birth, but who lived as women and had religious and medical roles within Scythian society. Given that the Scythians were expert horse breeders, it is entirely possible that the Enarees were castrated, though the story about them drinking the milk of pregnant mares as a source of oestrogen is a result of a misunderstanding of the historical texts.

Another example from the ancient world comes from the Roman historian Tacitus. Writing about the native peoples of the region Romans called Germania, he mentions a well-known sacred grove belonging to a tribe called the Nahanarvali who lived in what is now Poland (Tacitus). Here, he says, a pair of twin gods were worshipped by a male priest who wore women's clothing.

The Romans themselves also had a religious cult that involved gender transition. The goddess Cybele, whom the Romans called *Magna Mater* (the Great Mother) was popular throughout the empire. Numerous Roman sources attest that her worshippers included people called Galli who were assigned male at birth and who underwent ritual castration at their initiation, living as women thereafter. This was no minority cult; the head temple of the Cybele cult was on the Palatine Hill in Rome, close to the Imperial Palace (Beard, 1994). The Emperor Claudius made Cybele's main festival part of the official religious calendar, and therefore an empire-wide holiday.

Modern anthropologists have found evidence of cross-dressing shamans in tribal cultures as far apart as Argentina and Siberia. Such practices can still be found in many places around the world, including West Africa, Myanmar, and Chile.

There is no direct evidence of cross-dressing among the religious figures of ancient Western Europe. However, given how widespread the practice was, and the fact that the Cybele cult was popular in Roman Britain, it seems likely that the idea would have reach Britain's shores. In *Sistersong*, Lucy Holland re-imagines the wizard, Merlin, as a gender-fluid shaman who has blended druidic traditions with what might have been learned of the Galli, the Enarees, and similar groups known to the Classical world (Holland, 2021).

Another writer who has made use of this idea is Finland's Emmi Itäranta. Her latest novel, *The Moonday Letters*, is set in the 22nd century when mankind has fled the drowned Earth (Itäranta, 2022). Her central character, Lumi, is a professional healer whose techniques and knowledge hark back to an earlier culture. In conversation with her non-binary partner, Lumi notes:

Presenting gender outside the binary was sometimes seen as a sign of power and hidden abilities. Healers combined androgynous elements in their costumes, like a beard with a dress. They were believed to have greater insight into the world because they were not bound by one gender (p.191).

What does the prevalence of cross-dressing in tribal societies mean for religious belief? In part, any member of the tribe who is clearly different in some way might be seen as having a connection to the gods or the spirit world. The process of reproduction is also something that inevitably feeds into religious belief. The combination of a female person and a male person to make new human is a key aspect of life. In Hinduism the romantically paired gods, Shiva and Parvati, are symbolic of heterosexual love, but are sometimes depicted as a combined being, Ardhanarishvara, who is male on one side of the body and female on the other. The Roman god, Hermaphroditus, usually depicted as a woman with a penis, may have been of particular importance to couples about to marry.

One of the most interesting examples of this gender combination comes from the Inca. The indigenous peoples of Central and South America have a strong interest in matters of liminality and combination of opposites. According to one native source whose testimony was recorded by Spanish priests, there was a religious cult among the Inca called the quariwarmi (Morgan, 2017b). This is a Quechua word literally meaning "man-woman", which the Spanish translated as "hermaphrodite". They worshipped a god called Chuqui-Chinchay, the Rainbow Jaguar. As the quariwarmi connected male and female, so the rainbow connected Heaven and Earth. This sort of theology can easily be used to create a social space for gender diverse people when worldbuilding a religion.

So much for gender diversity, but were there actual gay or lesbian gods in human history? Well, in societies where same-sex relations were commonplace, of course there were. In ancient Greece it was traditional for a young man to be apprenticed to an older man who would act as a tutor, but would expect sexual favours in return. The exact age at which teenage boys would enter into such relationships, and at what point it would become sexual, is a matter of considerable debate amongst Classicists, but the relationship, known as pederasty, seems worryingly exploitative to modern eyes.

One of the most disturbing examples of this in Greek myth is the tale of Zeus and Ganymede. Zeus, who is a serial rapist of women, also kidnapped a beautiful young boy who would serve as his cup bearer. We know from Roman sources that such relationships could be sexual. The pub in Oxford at which the Inklings met is called the Eagle and Child, because its sign depicts Zeus, in the form of an eagle, kidnapping Ganymede.

Such relationships, however, seem to have been largely the preserve of the very wealthy. Pederasty usually involved a boy who had at least started puberty, and the relationship involved training and protection. When he embarked with Jason on the Argo, the god Heracles took with him a young man called Hylas (Apollonius). It is clear that Heracles and Hylas were a pederastic couple, though sadly for Heracles his handsome young lover was stolen away by nymphs during the voyage.

The point here, though, is that neither of these gods are minor figures in the Graeco-Roman pantheon. Zeus is symbolic of patriarchal power, and does all of the awful things powerful men do. Heracles, on the other hand, is a brave young hero. There are more depictions of Heracles than anyone else on Greek vases. His bisexuality was unremarkable to the Greeks and Romans. Marvel Comics have accepted this (Ching, 2015), and now that Heracles has been introduced to the MCU (under his Roman name of Hercules) we can hope to see that reflected in the movies (Waititi, 2022).

Fortunately for Heracles, he had other men in his life. One example is his nephew, Iolaus. The *Hercules* TV series (Raimi, 1995-99) didn't make much of their relationship, but the myths are clearer. Iolaus helped out on several of the famous Labours. According to legend, he hailed from the city of Thebes, and because of his association with the hero god he ended up being worshipped there. In the Classical era, Thebes was famous for an elite military unit made up of 150 pairs of male lovers. They were known as the Sacred Band, and their affection for each other was said to be a major reason for their effectiveness. They destroyed the mighty Spartan army at the Battle of Leuctra in 371 BCE, and were a major military power in Greece until they came up against Alexander's father, Philip II of Macedon, at the Battle of Chaeronea in 338 BCE (Romm, 2022).

The name "Sacred Band" suggests a religious aspect to these famous warriors. Contemporary sources are unclear on what this meant, but the Roman writer Plutarch, writing some 400 years later, claimed that the members of the band pledged their love for each other at the tomb of Iolaus. In *The Tangled Lands*, a forthcoming novel by Glenda Larke from Wizard's Tower Press, military units, both male and female, are selected solely from people who are same-sex attracted. Those who follow the war god, Saffrin, are described as being "saffrine" in their sexuality.

The other well-known pagan mythology in European tradition is that of the Norse. Here again gender ambiguity is associated with magic. Loki, of course, is as gender-fluid as they come. Although he is normally described as male, he is said to have spent a considerable amount of time as female (including time as a female horse, during which she gave birth to Odin's eight-legged steed, Sleipnir).

Loki's extreme gender-fluidity appears to have been associated with his command of magic. In one story Loki accuses Odin of cross-dressing. More precisely, he accuses the chief god of being "ergi", a word which suggests effeminacy and deviant sexuality (Larrington, 2008). Odin apparently did this to learn the secrets of seidr, a form of magic associated with femininity and overseen by the goddess Freya. Although seidr was traditionally practiced by women, it was also practiced by cross-dressed men. Olaf Tryggvason, the first Norwegian king to convert to Christianity, is said to have executed a group of seidr-men.

In the second book of his Magnus Chase and the Gods of Asgard series, *Magnus Chase and the Hammer of Thor*, Rick Riordan introduces a character whose father is human and whose mother is Loki (Riordan, 2017). Alex is gender-fluid, and flips between male and female pronouns at several points during the narrative. The hero, Magnus, is initially confused by this, but by the end of the book he has learned to read Alex's character and uses the correct pronouns naturally. By the end of the third book, Alex and Magnus are in a relationship (Fandom.com).

Gender changes also occur in Hindu mythology. The Tamil version of the Mahabharata includes the story of a brave young prince and his marriage to Krishna (Chowdhury, 2015). According to the story, Krishna's army is due to engage the forces of the enemy. A prophecy reveals that Krishna and his men will triumph, but only if one of the leaders of the army gives his life as a sacrifice to Kali. Aravan agrees to be the sacrifice, on condition of receiving three boons. The first is that his death should be a noble one in battle. The second is that he should live to see the war won. And the third is that he should be married before he dies. None of the local nobility are willing to marry a daughter to a man fated to die soon, so Krishna transforms himself into his female aspect, Mohini, and marries Aravan.

To this day, some trans women in Tamil Nadu join a religious cult that worships Aravan. They are known as Aravani. The high point of their religious year is a festival in the village of Koovagam where the marriage of Aravan and Mohini is re-enacted (John, 2013). The trans women play the part of Mohini. These days the festival is also an important celebration of trans rights in the region, and trans women from all over India travel to Koovagam for the festival. I don't know of any fiction which makes use of this story which is, after all, very much part of a living religion. However, it is a very clear example of how trans people can be incorporated into religious practices.

If you get your information about ancient religions from the internet you may have heard of a gay Aztec god called Xōchipilli, the Flower Prince. Sometimes the internet is the only easily accessible source of such information, because academic texts are so expensive and/or out of print. However, in this case we have some expert information to refer to. Author David O. Bowles has a side line in explaining the culture of the ancient Mesoamericans to white audiences, and has a whole article (Bowles, 2019) on the queerness and queer gods of the Nahuas (as we should more properly call the Aztecs).

According to Bowles, the Nahuas, like the Inca, were very much concerned with the unification of opposites. Xōchipilli and his sister, Xōchiqetzal, are more properly understood as two halves of a single gender-fluid being. They are gods of sexuality and gender expression (as well as of psychotropic drugs).

Buddhism is perhaps not the place you would look for gender-fluidity, yet it provides one of the most unusual examples. In ancient India, Buddhists worshipped a male bodhisattva known as Avalokiteśvara who represented compassion. As Buddhism spread through South-East Asia, this deity transformed into Guanyin, the goddess of mercy. Precisely how this happened is unclear. Possibly it was a translation issue, or perhaps Chinese culture was more comfortable with a female deity in that role.

The British Museum exhibition on feminine power presented Guanyin as gender-fluid as a standard part of their character, and even suggests that they/them pronouns might be appropriate. This is clearly a huge step for the Museum, but I'm not convinced that it is an accurate representation of ancient beliefs. What is clear is that Guanyin is now seen as iconic by modern-day queer folks, particularly those of South-East Asian ancestry. Religion evolves.

Recently, Guanyin was mentioned briefly in the Marvel TV series *She-Hulk: Attorney at Law* (Hunter, 2022). As part of a court case, Jennifer Walters and Wong have to rely on the testimony of a girl called Madisynn, who is rarely sober. As she takes the stand, Wong utters a quick prayer to Guanyin for "extra mercy". There is no mention of Guanyin's gender-fluid status in the show, but there can be little doubt that the Sorcerer Supreme is aware of it. Maybe we will find out more one day.

Finding examples of the use of such tales in contemporary fantasy is hard, but the ancients have given us plenty of actual examples. The *Epic of Gilgamesh* and the *Iliad* both contain good material for anyone who wants to do a gay love story, as Madeline Miller did with *The Song of Achilles* (Miller, 2011). For our purposes, a more interesting example is *Wrath Goddess Sing* by Maya Deane (Deane, 2022) which re-imagines Achilles as a trans woman. This might seem completely off the wall, but there is an actual myth in which Achilles' mother, Thetis, tries to save her son from his fated death in the Trojan War by dressing him as a girl and sending him to an elite boarding school for Greek princesses. Deane simply asks 'what if that was a choice made by Achilles rather than by Thetis?'

We can return now to the goddess Inanna/Ishtar and her genderqueer cultists. The most famous myth featuring Inanna is the one in which she visits her sister Ereshkigal, who is Queen of the Dead. Things go badly between the sisters and Inanna ends up dead. This is a disaster for the world of the living, because she is, amongst other things, the goddess of fertility. Without her, nothing can procreate.

So, the gods have to mount a rescue. They do so by sending two of Inanna's cultists down to the Underworld, because it turns out that Ereshkigal is a unable to resist the charms of cute gay boys who can sing and dance well. When she offers them a reward for their performance, they ask that Inanna be restored to life. Things don't necessarily go well for our heroes. In the Babylonian version of the myth (where there is only one rescuer), Ereshkigal curses gay men to forever be social outcasts, but the Sumerians seem to have been more open to diverse sexuality (Morgan, 2017a). Mythic retellings are all the rage these days. Someone should write the story from the point of view of those lads.

Despite this fashion, however, I found it quite difficult to find good examples of queer gods in contemporary science fiction and fantasy. A clear part of the problem is the question of what we mean by religion. Here are a few examples of "gods" in genre fiction.

In Roger Zelazny's Hugo-winning classic novel *Lord of Light*, the super-powered leaders of a colony spaceship successfully take on the aspects of Hindu gods (Zelazny, 2010). This allows them to subjugate the non-human inhabitants of the planet they hope to colonise, and leads them to being worshipped as gods by their human passengers.

A similar trick is pulled by the creators of the generation ship known as the Whorl in Gene Wolfe's Book of the Long Sun series (Wolfe, 1994-97). Typhon and his associates have uploaded their minds into the ship's computer system. The central character of the series, Pastor Silk, is a clergyman who serves one of the shrines where worshippers can hope to see the gods manifest on computer screens.

Julian May's Pliocene Exile (May, 1982-84) series sees a group of time travellers head back into Earth's deep past in search of peace, only to find the planet has been visited by powerful aliens. Our heroes make use of both alien and earthly futuristic technology, and end up becoming archetypes on which later religions will be based.

N. K. Jemisin's *The Hundred Thousand Kingdoms* includes a number of beings that are described as gods, but they are being held captive by the Arameri family in the cloud city of Sky, and are used as a source of power (Jemisin, 2010). They may be worshipped by the ordinary inhabitants of the empire that the Arameri rule, but they certainly aren't in Sky.

In Tamsyn Muir's The Locked Tomb series (Muir, 2020-22), John Gaius and his Lyctors are often described as having godlike powers, and compared to ordinary humans they do. However, by the end of *Nona the Ninth*, it has become clear that they were once ordinary humans who have acquired their powers through mastery of necromancy.

In Roz Kaveney's Rhapsody of Blood series, it is possible to become a god if you persuade your followers to kill enough people on your behalf (Kaveney, 2012-20). The series is about those ambitious people who aspire to godhood, and those who dedicate their lives to stopping them.

In Marvel comics, and the Marvel Cinematic Universe, the Asgardians are long-lived, super-powered aliens who became worshipped as gods by the ancient Norse inhabitants of Earth.

The common thread running throughout all of these examples is that the "gods" are not actually gods in the way that the gods of Christianity, Islam, and so on are gods. Rather, they are super-powered beings who are occasionally mistaken for gods by the less powerful. Whilst a valid view of the world, this is a book about religion and as such we should be discussing actual examples of worship of divine beings, not examples of mistaken veneration of powerful but non-divine beings.

My guess is that we got this way because the source material for most of our knowledge of polytheistic religion is from mythology, not from sacred texts. A myth is a story told about the gods, perhaps with the intention of making them understandable and relatable by humanising them. Many myths are explicit in stating that the gods in question have taken human form to walk among us, thought they are actually very far from human.

To understand why this doesn't work as a representation of religion, consider the example of the Gospels in the New Testament. In these books, Jesus has taken the form of a mortal man and lives among ordinary humans, occasionally doing miracles. We could take the view that these are myths told about Jesus, but if we then concluded that Jesus was simply a powerful magician with the ability to heal sickness and turn water into wine, we would be doing a great disservice to the Christian religion. We should allow the same respect to the adherents of the polytheistic religions of the past.

Incidentally, science fiction has done the same thing to Jesus as it does to other gods. Michael Moorcock's *Behold the Man* features a time traveller who goes into the past to meet Jesus, and ends up becoming the man about whom the Gospels are written (Moorcock, 1969). Interestingly from our point of view, one of the reasons that Karl Glogauer wants to meet Jesus is because he is troubled by his homosexual feelings.

One way in which writers have tried to make their gods more god-like is to make them personifications of natural forces. In Moorcock's Eternal Champion books there are beings known as the Lords of Law and Chaos (Moorcock, 1962-2008). This skewing of the axis of good and evil, which found its way into immortality via *Dungeons and Dragons*, presents a much less moralistic view of the universe. The Lords of Chaos, because of their nature, break all human social taboos, including those around sex and gender.

Another example is given by the Endless in Neil Gaiman's Sandman (Gaiman, 1989-2020). This family of immortal beings includes Death, Delirium, Desire, Despair, Destiny, Destruction, and Dream. They spend most of their time fulfilling their function as living embodiments of the concepts they represent. While they are not actually worshipped very much, they do feel far more like divine beings than most of the "gods" in comic books. Desire, because of their nature, is as fluid in sexuality and gender as any of the Lords of Chaos, and is splendidly portrayed by the non-binary actor, Mason Alexander Park, in the Netflix TV series (Gaiman, 2022).

The other problem I had finding good examples of queer gods in genre literature was that the portrayals I found were almost always negative. Our ability to understand how gender and sexuality was viewed in ancient, polytheistic religions has been undermined by 19th century historians who tended to view anything pagan as perverted. Hence, we find frequent references to "temple prostitutes" when there is no convincing evidence that such people existed. What ancient references we do have tend to come from Greeks and Romans writing at some distance in time from what they are describing, and who are often as prudish as their more modern counterparts.

Nevertheless, the idea that gods who are involved with sex—especially non-procreative, outside-of-marriage sex—are somehow perverted has found its way into fiction. The association of queerness with evil, or at least with deviance, persists. When I asked people on Twitter for good examples of gay gods, people enthusiastically recommended Tanith Lee's *Night's Master* (1978). The bisexual god in that book is the Azhrarn; the Prince of Demons.

One of the more impressive attempts to create an actual polytheistic religion in a fantasy world is Lois McMaster Bujold's World of the Five Gods series (Bujold, 2001-2016). These were also warmly recommended to me by people on Twitter, because there is actually a gay god in the books. However, this god is literally called "The Bastard". What's more, there is a heretical sect that regards him as a demon rather than one of the five gods.

Part of the problem is that straight adults today are still often conditioned to see queer sex as deviant and therefore bad, and therefore don't see any problem with the only representation of queerness in the divine as being tainted with evil. However, this does not necessarily reflect the reality of real pagan religion. Sure, Loki is morally dubious, but Heracles is a great hero. Our queer gods don't always have to be like Loki.

One possible way out of this is through people from non-Western cultures writing their own books based on their own religions. An example is *David Mogo, Godhunter* (Okunbowa, 2019) by Suyi Davies Okungbowa. This is near future science fiction set in Lagos, but it makes heavy use of West African traditional religion. These gods are known as Orisha, and the pantheons differ somewhat depending on which ethnic group in West Africa we are talking about, or indeed if we are looking at the African diaspora in Brazil, the Caribbean, and the USA.

Okunbowa's gods include Olókun, the god of the sea, who is canonically multi-gendered in the real-world religion. We can pair that with Akwaeke Emezi's Otherwise Award-winning *Freshwater* (Emezi, 2019), which uses West African ideas of spiritual possession to help explain a trans identity, and with Rita Indiana's *Tentacle* (Indiana, 2018), which also features Olókun. Nalo Hopkinson makes good use of the Voudou Loa, Erzulie, in her Sandman universe comic, *House of Whispers* (2018-20). As goddess of love, Erzulie is decidedly unworried about who she has sex with. Another solution is, of course, for queer people to write the books. I note that Rita Indiana, Akwaeke Emezi, and Nalo Hopkinson all identify as queer in various ways.

But perhaps we can do away with gods altogether. Many modern pagans focus more on spirituality and a connection with nature than on the worship of gods. Such people may be drawn to books such as Robert Holdstock's *Mythago Wood*, which owes much of its success to the way in which it evokes the spirit of the wild wood (Holdstock, 1984).

Modern pagans write fantasy too. The most famous example is possibly the Illuminatus! trilogy by Robert Shea and Robert Anton Wilson (Shea & Wilson, 1975). Those books were based heavily on the activities of neo-pagans from the San Francisco Bay Area with whom the authors were familiar. Shea, Wilson, and their friends did not take their religion entirely seriously, and their crowning achievement was probably helping inspire Bill Drummond to create the massively successful electronic dance band, the KLF. The band was also known as the Justified Ancients of Mu Mu, which is a direct reference to the Illuminatus! books.

Other, more serious, pagans have also written fantasy. Possibly the most famous is the occultist Dion Fortune. In works such as *The Sea Priestess*, she has sought to portray pagan religion and working systems of magic (Fortune, 1938).

Rachel Pollack is less famous as an occultist, but better known as an expert on the tarot than as a novelist. Her Clarke Award winning novel, *Unquenchable Fire*, is heavily rooted in her understanding of modern paganism (Pollack, 1989).

Liz Williams is the best-known current practitioner of both paganism and fantasy. Her current series about the four Fallow sisters is very much concerned with pagan themes, though mostly with the existence of supernatural beings rather than actual gods. However, the most recent book, *Embertide*, features a character who, in the world of the book, had been worshipped in Roman London (Williams, 2022).

Dr. Graham Harvey, a lecturer in Religious Studies at the Open University who specialises in studying modern paganism, has found fantasy fiction a rich source of material. In his view, one of the writers who best encapsulates the spirit of modern paganism in their work is Sir Terry Pratchett (Harvey, 2000). I understand that Pratchett was once initiated into Wicca, but as his career took off, he became too busy to take an active part in the religion.

Of course, modern paganism—just like the rest of the modern world—is prone to queerphobia. The Goddess Movement in particular, with its focus on the divine power of femininity, is prone to biological essentialism and therefore transphobia. This has been the case at least as far back as the early 1990s when Neil Gaiman wrote a transphobic moon goddess into his Sandman story, *A Game of You* (Gaiman, 1993). Gaiman originally intended the story to be a criticism of transphobia in paganism, but sadly it has been widely and incorrectly interpreted as proof that he is transphobic.

Clearly what we need here is queer pagans who are also science fiction or fantasy writers. I'm sure they are out there, and I'm looking forward to reading the new epic fantasy series from Tej Turner, The Avatars of Ruin (Turner, 2021).

I should end by asking whether there is any scope for queerness in books that are based on Christianity, and the answer is a resounding 'YES!' Mediaeval Christianity is queerer than we have been led to believe.

One of the most remarkable books to come out of the mediaeval world is *Le Roman de Silence*, written in Old French and attributed to one Heldris de Cornuälle (Heldris of Cornwall). It tells the tale of a young person assigned female at birth but who is raised as a boy and becomes a famous knight. The book is shot through with internal debates in which personifications of "nature" and "nurture" discuss the benefits of the male and female genders. The book has been turned into a modern YA fantasy novel, *The Story of Silence*, by Alex Myers (Myers, 2020).

Muslims hold that God is both male and female (though they use male pronouns when forced to by gendered languages), because if God were only male then there would be something that God was not, and therefore God would not be omnipotent. Christian theologians have tackled this issue too, and Michelangelo, when painting the Sistine Chapel, produced one image of God which has a pronounced bust. In that picture, God is in the process of creation, which the painter clearly saw as something requiring a feminine principle.

Mediaeval theologians also wrestled with the question of whether Jesus, being God, might also be part-female. Images of the wound that Jesus received from a Roman spear while hanging on the cross are common in mediaeval art, and often those images look suspiciously like a vulva, which also bleeds (Spencer-Hall & Gutt, 2021).

For an example in literature, we can go to the Cornish *Ordinalia*, a set of mystery plays which are the oldest surviving works in the Cornish language. Mystery plays are about the life of Jesus, and the Cornish, for obvious reasons, have always been interested in mermaids. In one of the plays, as part of the trial of Jesus before Pontius Pilate, one of the lawyers comments that not only is Jesus half-man and half-god, but He is also half-woman just like a mermaid (Haroian, 1989).

So there we have it. God, or at least some of Them, is undoubtedly queer, and always has been. It is perfectly possible for science fiction and fantasy to portray queer religions. However, in order to do so, writers need to get away from various 19th century ideas. They need to accept polytheistic and animistic religions as theologically valid, and they need to accept queerness as something natural and normal, not a product of "evil" gods. Authors are always looking for ideas, right?

Bibliography

Apollonius. *Argonautica*.

Beard, M., 1994. The Roman and the Foreign; The Cult of the 'Great Mother' in Imperial Rome. *Shamanism, History, and the State*. Michigan: University of Michigan Press.

Bowles, D.O., 2019. *Mexican X Part XII: Xochihuah and Queer Aztecs*. [online] Available at: <https://davidbowles.medium.com/mexican-x-part-xii-what-did-a-xochihuah-possess-3784532d8023>.

Bujold, L.M., 2001-2016. *The World of the Five Gods* series, comprising 14 novels and novellas, New York: Eos and Wake Forest, NC: Baen.

Ching, A., July 2015. *Marvel Addresses "Hercules'" Sexuality*. [online] Available at: <https://www.cbr.com/marvel-addresses-hercules-sexuality/>.

Chowdhury, S., January 2016. The Tragic Story Of Aravan: Origin Of The Third Gender. [online] Available at: <https://www.boldsky.com/yoga-spirituality/anecdotes/2015/tragic-story-of-aravan-origin-of-the-third-gender-060821.html>.

Deane, M., 2022. *Wrath Goddess Sing*. New York: William Morrow.

Emezi, A., 2019. *Freshwater*. London: Faber & Faber.

Enheduanna. Passionate Inanna. [online] Available at <https://etcsl.orinst.ox.ac.uk/cgi-bin/etcsl.cgi?text=t.4.07.3#>

Fandom.com, n.d. [online] Available at: <https://riordan.fandom.com/wiki/Alex_Fierro>.

Fortune, D., 1938. *The Sea Priestess*. Wellingborough, England: The Aquarian Press.

Gaiman, N., 1989-2020. *The Sandman* comic book. New York: DC Comics and Vertigo.
---, 1993. *The Sandman: A Game of You*. New York: Vertigo.

Haroian, G., 1989. The Cornish Mermaid: The Fine Thread of Androgyny in the 'Ordinalia'. *Medieval & Renaissance Drama in England* 4: 1–11. [online] Available at : http://www.jstor.org/stable/24322290.

Harvey, G., 2000. Paganism as observed and enhanced by Terry Pratchett. *Journal of the British Association for the Study of Religions*. [online] Available at: <http://jbasr.com/basr/diskus/diskus1-6/harvey-6.txt>.

Helle, S., 2022. *Gilgamesh: A New Translation of the Ancient Epic*. Yale: Yale University Press.

Hercules: The Legendary Journeys, 1995-1999. [films] Directed by Sam Raimi. USA: Renaissance Pictures.

Herodotus. *The Histories*, translated by Aubrey De Sélincourt. London: Penguin.

Holdstock, R., 1984. *Mythago Wood*. London: Gollancz.

Holland, L., 2021. *Sistersong*. London: Macmillan.

Hopkinson, N., 2018-20. *House of Whispers* comics. New York: DC Black Label.

Indiana, R., 2018. *Tentacle And Other Stories*. Sheffield: And Other Stories.

Itäranta, E., 2022. *The Moonday Letters*. London: Titan.

Jemisin, N.K., 2010. *The Hundred Thousand Kingdoms*. New York: Orbit.

John, S.S., 2013. *Under the Full Moon: The Aravan Fest*. Indira Gandhi National Centre for the Arts. [online] Available at: <https://archive.org/details/dli.Aravan.Fest>.

Kaveney, R., 2012-20. The Rhapsody of Blood series, currently comprising *Rituals* (2012), *Reflections* (2013), *Resurrections* (2014) & *Realities* (2020). San Francisco: Plus One Press.

Larrington, C., 2008. *The Poetic Edda*. Oxford: Oxford World's Classics.

Lee, T., 1978. *Night's Master*. New York: DAW.

May, J., 1982-84. The Saga of the Pliocene Exiles, comprising *The Many Coloured Land* (1982), *The Golden Torc* (1982), *The Non-Born King* (1983) & *The Adversary* (1984). London: Pan.

Miller, M., 2011. *The Song of Achilles*. London: Bloomsbury.

Moorcock, M., 1969. *Behold the Man*. London: Allison & Busby.
---, 1962-2008. The Eternal Champion series, comprising over 50 novels in a shared universe. London: Gollancz.

Morgan, C., 2017a. *Evidence for Trans Lives in Sumer*. [online] Available at: <https://notchesblog.com/2017/05/02/evidence-for-trans-lives-in-sumer/>.
---, 2017b. Trans People in the Inca Empir. *Gendered Voices* #2. [online] Available at: <https://issuu.com/swwdtpgenderandsexualityresearch/docs/gendered_20voices_20issue_20two-_20>.

Muir, T., 2020-22. The Locked Tomb series, currently comprising *Gideon the Ninth*

(2020), *Harrow the Ninth* (2021) & *Nona the Ninth* (2022). New York: Tor.com.

Myers, A., 2020. *The Story of Silence*. New York: Harper Voyager.

Okungbowa, S.D:, 2019. *David Mogo, Godhunter*. Oxford: REBCA.

Pollack, R., 1989. *Unquenchable Fire*. London: Orbit.

Riordan, R., 2017. *Magnus Chase and the Hammer of Thor*. London: Puffin.

Romm, J., 2022. *The Sacred Band: Three Hundred Theban Lovers and the Last Days of Greek Freedom*. New York: Simon & Schuster.

She-Hulk: Attorney at Law, 2022, episode 4. [series] Available through: Disney Plus [Accessed August-October 2022].

Shea, R., & Wilson, R.A., 1975. The Illuminatus! trilogy, comprising *The Eye in the Pyramid*, *The Golden Apple* & *Leviathan*. New York: Dell.

Spencer-Hall, A. & Gutt B. (eds.), 2021. *Trans and Genderqueer Subjects in Mediaeval Hagiography*. Amsterdam: Amsterdam University Press.

Tacitus. *Germania*. Available from Project Gutenberg: <https://www.gutenberg.org/files/7524/7524-h/7524-h.htm>

The Sandman, 2022. [series] Available through: Netflix [Accessed 1 October 2022].

Thor: Love and Thunder, 2022. [film] Directed by Taika Waititi. USA: Marvel Studios.

Turner, T., 2021-22. The Avatars of Ruin series, currently comprising *Bloodsworn* (2021) and *Blood Legacy* (2022). England: Elsewhen Press.

Williams, L., 2022. *Embertide*. England: NewCon Press.

Wolfe, G., 1994-97. The Book of the Long Sun series, comprising *Nightside of the Long Sun* (1994), *Lake of the Long Sun* (1994), *Caldé of the Long Sun* (1995) & *Exodus from the Long Sun* (1997). London: Hodder.

Zelazny, R., 2010. *Lord of Light*. London: Gollancz SF Masterworks.

"This is my story" - Girardian Theory and the Christian Subtext of *Final Fantasy X*

Giovanni Carmine Costabile

Abstract

The major trend in the scholarship and general opinion concerning the 2001 Squaresoft role-playing videogame *Final Fantasy X* (*FFX*) has always been inclined towards an antireligious, antitheistic view of the game in all of its narratological, worldbuilding, ludological, and even musicological aspects. According to Sjølie, from an "analysis of both the narratological and ludological design of *Final Fantasy*", one infers that the "rhetoric in the game essentially suggests to the player that a world free of religion is the ultimate goal, and will eventually save the world" (2018, p.63), so coming "to the conclusion that the game carries elements of both Nietzschean and Marxian theories regarding religious critique" (p.63). Even in his 2017 MM thesis on the musicology of the *Hymn of the Fayth*, Greenfield-Casas declares without compromise that his field of inquiry will be "*FFX*'s overtly antitheistic storyline that ends in deicide" (p.5). However, Caldwell in 2013 had argued that "*Final Fantasy X* uses its social framing of religion to provide the potential for religious education, which is a different but still potent form of religious experience" (58), and in 2015 even added that the game "is one of the most compelling examples yet of video games' potential as spheres of religious experience" (p.160). My proposal entails the application of René Girard's theory of the scapegoat to the sacrificial narrative of *FFX* to shed light on the Christian subtext of a videogame only superficially readable as antireligious, instead proving itself a foreshadowing of the overt Christology of *Final Fantasy XV*.

Introduction: What is *Final Fantasy X* about?

Writing a good synopsis of the fictitious background underlying the plot of the 2001 Squaresoft role-playing videogame *Final Fantasy X* (*FFX*) is a task way more demanding than one may suppose, but knowledge of what lies behind the scenes is fundamental to understand the game plot, so I offer my take.

About 1,000 years ago, in the world of Spira, a war broke out between the cities of Zanarkand and Bevelle: the former relied on the power of its summoners, the latter on advanced technology and the skill of its builders. As the technological superiority of Bevelle allowed the city to get the advantage in the conflict, the sovereign and high summoner of Zanarkand, Yu Yevon, could not help but take refuge on the slopes of Mount Gagazet, together with the few survivors. Despite the dire moment, Yu Yevon would not accept the defeat of his city. Therefore, he transformed the survivors into fayth, statues inhabited by undead souls. The fayth would always dream of Zanarkand, therefore preserving the memory of the splendor of the city. In order to protect the dream, Yevon created Sin, a gigantic leviathan-like entity shaped by attracting a huge amount of spirits called "pyreflies". Yu Yevon gave Sin one job: to preserve the dream of the fayth, preventing any human group from reaching a population and technological progress so great that they could endanger the refuge of the fayth. From this moment on, Sin began to spread terror in Spira. Meanwhile, Yunalesca, daughter of Yu Yevon, and Zaon, her husband, had managed to escape on the eve of the final battle, and had thus escaped the destruction of Zanarkand. After a certain period of time, Yunalesca made an agreement with the leader of Bevelle. In exchange for the revelation of a way to defeat Sin, she asked for perennial adoration from the entire world towards her father. The leader of Bevelle was afraid of Sin's power, so he accepted, and Yunalesca embarked on her journey to the ruins of Zanarkand: there the summoner was able to defeat Sin for the first time, transforming her husband Zeon into an Aeon, and sacrificing him. However, after some time, Yu Yevon managed to take control of Zaon, and used him as a core to regenerate Sin. Yunalesca, bound by the promise made to Bevelle, remained in Zanarkand. From there, she would continue to provide a way to defeat Sin. However, after a long time, no one had completed the task successfully, so Yunalesca created the Fayth of the Temples. By visiting them, the bravest could become familiar with the art of summoning, and prepare for the summoning of the Final Aeon. Spira lived for centuries in the false hope that one day Sin would not return, but Yu Yevon would always possess the Final Aeon, and generate a new Sin.

Although the player only discovers the whole picture of such events little by little throughout the unfolding of the game, it is preferable to adopt a chronological approach in explaining such a setting to the general reader. The extent of the full synopsis in two parts also helps in doing justice to the complexity of the gaming experience.

The actual game begins in Zanarkand, celebrating the blitzball final which will be attended by Tidus, star of the team and son of the famous champion Jecht, who unfortunately mysteriously disappeared about ten years earlier. Everything seems to be going well until Sin devastates the metropolis. During the attack, Tidus makes the acquaintance of the elusive Auron. Before even realizing what is going on, Tidus is soon sucked into a dimensional vortex. When the protagonist wakes up, he finds himself alone in the vicinity of some submerged ruins in the middle of the ocean, to then meet Rikku, a girl belonging to the Al Bhed race, who will explain to him that Zanarkand was destroyed 1000 years ago. Hence Tidus deduces that he is now in the future. However, the two are again attacked by Sin and the protagonist wakes up on Besaid beach, where he meets Wakka, captain of a blitzball team. Getting to the village he will also meet the powerful black sorceress Lulu, then he enters the temple unauthorized, there to meet Yuna, an apprentice summoner and daughter of the High Summoner Braska, accompanied by her guardian Kimahri. Yuna wins the trial of the fayth and summons her first Aeon, Valefor. Destiny is therefore in the hands of the young and sweet Yuna, who will start a pilgrimage in order to obtain the help of the other Aeons, the only ones who can help her in defeating Sin. Once they leave, however, they are attacked by Sin, who destroys the village of Kilika. All Yuna can do is to perform the rite of Sending to prevent the poor souls, consumed by anger, from turning into monsters. The group, thereafter joined also by Auron and Rikku, travels to all the chief Yevon temples throughout Spira, so that Yuna may commune with the fayth sealed in a statue at each place and collect support from all the Aeons. During their pilgrimage, the company repeatedly meets a sinister High Priest called Seymour, who proposes to Yuna but secretly harbors mad thoughts to lay waste to all Spira. After Tidus rescues Yuna from the combined marriage on the very day of the wedding before the rite is sealed, Tidus and Yuna fall in love, so that Tidus tries to convince her not to give up her life for the higher cause, not even to honour her father. In fact, little by little he comes to learn the truth about Sin, in search for information useful to save his beloved. So, the more is discovered, the more the church of Yevon is revealed to be hypocritical and corrupt, shedding radical doubt on the system of belief underlying the entire civilized world on Spira. But also more is revealed. Together with Jecht and Braska, Auron had already participated in the destruction of Sin, but had lost his life, killed by Yunalesca, following the attempt to avenge his two friends who had died in the battle against Sin. After his death, however, as an unsent he was able, traveling through Sin, to reach Dream Zanarkand in order to keep a promise made to Jecht, the father of Tidus, to take care of the child. As predicted by Auron, Sin also showed up ten years later in Dream Zanarkand and razed the city to the ground during a game of blitzball in which Tidus was also playing. Sin's force then generates a space-time tunnel that drags Auron and Tidus out of Dream Zanarkand of the fayth. Such a discovery entails that Sin's end would erase Tidus from existence as well, because he is only a dream of the fayth. In fact, when the company meets Yunalesca in the ruins of real Zanarkand, Yuna is finally convinced that Tidus is right and she decides that she refuses to summon the Final Aeon because nobody has to die. Together with Cid of the Al Bhed, they devise and enact a plan to get inside Sin and kill Yu Yevon, after which not only Sin, Dream Zanarkand and the Aeons fade away, but also Tidus, evaporating in his last embrace of his beloved Yuna, who is left astonished. Spira is now free from both the torment of its bane and the lies demanding lives for a false hope.

The actual gaming experience of *FFX* involves much more than any synopsis, however extensive, may enucleate, but at least any reader may get an idea of what the game's plot is concerned with.

Is *Final Fantasy X* antireligious (and anticlerical)?

As I narrated above, as the game plot unfolds and more is discovered, the more the church of Yevon is revealed to be hypocritical and corrupt, shedding radical doubt on the system of belief underlying the entire civilized world on Spira. Such elements led many players and even critics to believe that *FFX* is an antireligious game. Kristofer Fjøsne Sjølie believes that "*Final Fantasy X*'s procedural religion express[es] a rhetoric of no-religion" (2018, p.V), so that it is clear how it purports that "religious ideas such as sacrifice, martyrdom and tradition are not the correct way to solve the deeper issues that exists in the game's reality", and, ultimately, "the game essentially suggests to the player that a world free of religion is the ultimate goal, and will eventually save the world" (p.63). The association with Nietzsche, together with Machiavelli, had already been proposed in 2009 by David Hahn in his contribution to the (unauthorized) collection *Final Fantasy and Philosophy*. Even in a musicological analysis of the *Hymn of the Fayth* that could abstain from such comments, Greenfield-Casas argues that the ending of the game brings about "the 'end' of religion with the death of god" (2017, p.17). While comparing videogames in general to religions, he still maintains that, even in the context of "the (covertly) antitheistic architecture of most video games" (p.vii), *FFX* stands out for its "overtly antitheistic storyline that ends in deicide" (p.5). Nor is it an ideological/confessional prejudice, as for example Kevin Schut, in his 2013 book *Of Games and God: A Christian Exploration of Video Games*, writes that there is a "general hostility of many games towards religions, or perhaps more accurately, towards the church" (p.33), and of such tendencies "[a]nother example is *Final Fantasy X*, the plot of which revolves around a religion that the player eventually reveals to be a false front" (p.34).

From my point of view, it is not enough to say that all these interpretations are unconvincing; rather, I would like to affirm that the exact opposite from their statements is the truth, i.e. *FFX* is not only a deeply religious videoludical artwork imbued with strong Christian values, but it is even a profound meditation on the nature of religion in general and Christianity in particular, one that is founded on the reflections of René Girard and touches upon the very essence of the sacred and the deep core of the Gospel.

Or is *Final Fantasy X* religious (and Christian)?

To begin with, one might wonder, if the game was so decidedly antireligious or even antichristian, how could it be that, as it results from a 2010 survey among Christian gamers, "*Assassin's Creed* tied with *Final Fantasy* (Square Enix, 1987) with sixteen votes, the fifth most popular series" (Luft, 2014, p.159). Secondly, there are approaches to reading the game outside the controversy between religious and antireligious meaning altogether, like Washburn who instead sees as key the "relationship of memory, history, and the struggle for control of knowledge" (2009, p.151). Then, one might also wonder whether the Church of Yevon in the game should be simply taken to represent religion in general, or even whether its alleged association with Christianity altogether or the Catholic Church is indeed correct. In fact, in Peter Likarish's reconstruction, Yevon rather resembles the Luddites: "The details of Yevonism are a mishmash of several practiced religions, but an observant player of the game will tease out threads of Calvinism, Catholicism, and, of course, the beliefs of the Luddites" (Likarish, 2014, pp.176-177). Furthermore, Kyrie Eleison H. Caldwell observed how in Spira "[t[he temple plan, statues, and hymn recall Catholic cathedrals (...), while the runes resemble a classical Sanskrit script used in several Japanese and Indian Buddhist traditions that invoke deities through their Sanskrit initials" (Caldwell, 2015, pp.166-167), and William Huber pointed out that "[i]t may be appropriate to see references to national religion [in *FFX*] as a reflection of the so-called state Shinto in the Meiji period" (Huber, 2007, p.172). Just from a few observations we may see how complex the picture is, which is already a realization we should maintain before getting into the matter properly. Third, and finally, we should recall that we are not studying a treatise on organized religion, nor a novel, but a videogame, which requires an evaluation not only of the setting and plot, however much they are important components, but also of the gaming experience, which in this case simulates an entire pilgrimage of cultural and spiritual discovery the significance of which is not denied by the wrongs of the heads of Yevonite clergy as much as the invocations of the Aeons, the ritual of the Sending, and Sin are real in the game, and the deception of the church only concerns the way to handle the latter, besides being first of all self-deception. Thus it was that Caldwell in 2013 argued that "*Final Fantasy X* uses its social framing of religion to provide the potential for religious education, which is a different but still potent form of religious experience" (p.58), to later conclude that the game "is one of the most compelling examples yet of video games' potential as spheres of religious experience" (2015, p.160). Anthony J. Eisner took a further step in what I deem to be the right direction and compared *FFX* with Dostoevskij, comparing Yunalesca with the Grand Inquisitor and Tidus with Jesus as portrayed in the famous passage in *The Brothers Karamazov*. In his account, both the Grand Inquisitor and Yunalesca think that, being happiness and freedom in their opinion mutually exclusive, it is better for mankind at large to live in the small happiness of their false hope, remitting their freedom to their rulers, who will be the only ones to know the truth of things. That the false hope is the return of Jesus in Dostoevskij, and Sin's final defeat in Spira does not spoil the parallelism. On the contrary, the choice of freedom by Tidus is fundamentally the same as Jesus's when he resisted the three temptations in the desert by Satan, The Grand Inquisitor rebukes Jesus for refusing all three temptations, and in particular secular power, which is what his church is based on, like Yevon's cult in Spira. Like Jesus, furthermore, Tidus not only chooses freedom for himself, but also calls others to freedom, beginning from Yuna.

The comparison with Dostoevskij conducted by Eisner acutely highlights how, in spite of what Sjølie, Hahn, Greenfield-Casas, and Schut thought, a critique of religion, institutional or not, does not necessarily imply rejection of religion nor of institution. Dostoevskij wrote the extraordinary tale of the Grand Inquisitor but he put it in Ivan's words, who is not the main character. It is his brother Aleksej, a novice monk, who listens to Ivan's tale, and it is Aleksej who most closely represents the author, and it is Aleksej who, after the tale is over, imitates Jesus's kiss to the Grand Inquisitor in kissing his brother as a response. Dostoevskij's point of view is a believer's, not an atheist's or an agnostic's. Thus, even more crucially, Eisner observes:

> In "The Grand Inquisitor," Jesus gave only one answer to the Grand Inquisitor and that is the answer of Love. Jesus is told that Humanity is weak and cannot become free and happy and must choose between the two. However, it is the answer of love that revokes this, as love is what will bring humanity to make the good choice. Tidus is an example of this (...). It is love that allows Tidus to make the best decision in his hopelessness. His love for Yuna, and his love for his

friends will not allow him to accept fate as the only option that Yunalesca provides. Rather he searches for a better way to save the people he loves. It is also through love that Tidus sacrifices himself to create a free world for his friends. Knowing that defeating Sin/Yu Yevon will destroy the power that allows him to exist, he still strives for the best option he creates and decides upon. This is another similarity he has with Jesus as he sacrificed himself for the betterment of those that he loves. Through love, humanity will reject the temptations of the Grand Inquisitor. (Eisner, 2017, p.87)

Like the Gospel, then, *FFX* is fundamentally a love story, even though the actual relationship between Tidus and Yuna comes near the end and is brief. Also human general recognition of Jesus as the Messiah only lasted one day, on Palm Sunday, when his entrance in Jerusalem was acclaimed in great joy and with high praise, only a handful of days before crucifying him. The relationship between God and man has been often compared to a troubled love story already by Jews, and Christians reinterpreted it as love between Christ and his bride the Church. Certainly Yuna the priestess can work as a good image of such a churchly bride. After all, as Michal Daliot-Bul recalls the subway advertisement of *FFX* he saw in Tokyo in the summer of 2001:

The purity we have forgotten. . .
The characters in the game can now show with their eyes and expressions
that which people cannot express.
We have forgotten
Pure feelings, love.
The purity that makes us cry.
(Daliot-Bul, 2009, p.367)

There are certainly a variety of opinions on any subject, but I cannot see how purity could ever be seen as anything but a religious value. And, if the very commercial of the game aims at selling it by presenting it as a celebration of a religious value, I would think at least twice before cataloguing the game as "antireligious". Daliot-Bul also adds that he noticed a "blurring of distinctions" between real and imaginary characters in both the advertisement and the game itself, since Tidus is eventually revealed to be a dream, but then it will be useful to recall the mirror episode of Tidus's "death" in *Final Fantasy VII*, as Michelle K. Menard reports:

> *Final Fantasy VII* is referred to time and time again as having either the most shocking or saddest moment of video game history (...) when one of the villains, Sephiroth, impales the innocent Aeris as she prays to the planet for help. Players worldwide shouted foul as this important player character was killed off so quickly and unexpectedly. (…) A few years later, Square released another RPG often cited for its heartwrenching ending, *Final Fantasy X*. Here, Square took a Romeo-and-Juliet approach to the plot, foreshadowing the ending quite clearly through many of the main plot points, but giving the player a false sense of hope that he could indeed make a difference to the outcome. (…) [P]layers were moved often to tears by the doomed love story or sense of helplessness. (Menard, 2008, pp.13-14)

It can be seen that there is a pattern: an innocent character somehow involved with religion dies as a sacrifice to save the world. It is sheer Christlikeness, or nothing is nor may ever be. Nonetheless, in *Final Fantasy VII* there is no institutional religion, the Christlike figure is a woman, and it is not an immediate effect of her sacrifice to save the world. Thus it is *FFX* that is a closer image of Christianity, a fact the full significance of which shall be explained in its connection with Girardian theory.

Final Fantasy X and Girardian theory

René Girard (25 December 1923-4 November 2015) was a French philosophical anthropologist famous for his theories of the dynamics of mimetic desire and the scapegoat mechanism as neglected foundational stones of all civilization. Author of more than thirty volumes, among his most important books there are *La Violence et le sacré* (1972; *Violence and the Sacred*, 1977) and *Des choses cachées depuis la fondation du monde* (1978; *Things Hidden Since the Foundation of the World*, 1987). He taught at the State University of New York at Buffalo, the Johns Hopkins University at Baltimore, and Stanford University. He received several honorary degrees and his approach was so fruitful that in 1990 the Colloquium on Violence and Religion (COV&R) was founded, with a goal to explore topics related to violence, religion, scapegoating and mimetic theory. The first president and co-founder of the COV&R was the Roman Catholic theologian Raymund Schwager, and Girard was Honorary Chair. The John Templeton Foundation sponsors the Mimetic Theory Project for advanced research. In 2005 Girard was elected a member of the Académie Française.

Girardian theory of mimetic desire states that desire of any kind is not innate in humans but arises in imitation of other desiring subjects, so that there are always three parts: the subject of desire, the object, and the model after whom the subject developed desire for the object. It is then only consequential that a competition is inevitable between subject and model for possession of the object. Since the three of them are not alone, though, but live in a society, there are many of these triplets, and they often develop into quartets, quintuplets, etc., for others also imitate the original desire of the model, or the derivative desire of the subject, or they may even imitate the rivalry between subject and model instead, and so on, in chains as long as they may be. The result is an escalation of generalized violence and chaos that only allows one solution: the whole of the aggressiveness of the community must be polarized against a single, arbitrary victim, the scapegoat, who shall then be sacrificed so to appease everyone. In the light of the effectiveness of the victim's sacrifice in restoring peace, the scapegoat is often credited with the foundation of tribes, cities, kingdoms, or nations, and even worshipped as a god. Over time, the necessity to avoid escalations of violence whenever possible required the enforcement of both prohibitions of imitations, the so-called *taboos* (to control the insurgence of mimetic rivalries and their escalations) and prescriptions of imitations, called *rituals* (to limit and quell said escalations and their damages as well as the compensation they exact for their extinguishment). This mechanism is thus the founding stone of all civilization, the subject of all myth and the basis of all religion.

As a part of the mechanism, its functioning itself must remain hidden, however in plain sight: most ancient accounts of such lynchings are both told from the point of view of the lynchers (the community), and "romanticized". Orpheus is torn apart by the Menads, but that happened because he despised any woman who was not his Eurydice, and anyway he went to the happy fields of Elysium after death. Oedipus suffered the anger of the Thebans only because his sins had brought the plague upon the city, and anyway Zeus thereafter took him onto Olympus to live among gods. This way society can live with its constitutional guilt without it becoming conscious anguish and self-reprimand that might impede or get in the way of future lynchings whenever they may be again necessary to suppress uncontrolled escalations of violence once more arising from mimetic desire and rivalry.

Insofar, *FFX* is perfectly in line with Girardian theory. In the ancient past, Spira was entirely magical, that is, entirely mimetic, since Girard says that magic is a form of imitation. Then machines came into play, but how are they described but as an imitation of magic, since they were another way to do the same things? Indeed, the Machina Wars between Zanarkand and Bevelle may be presented as a war of magic against technology, but actually both sides use both, as it is stressed even more in the sequels *Final Fantasy X-2* and *Final Fantasy X-2.5*; however Zanarkand is stronger in magic and Bevelle in technology. So we have a past when mimetic competition escalated to full-scale total war, and the result was that a single man, Yu Yevon, sacrificed his whole community to preserve it as a memory. This might seem the opposite of the lynching, where instead it is everybody against one, but Girard contemplates this case too, as he replies to the objection: "There are also myths in which no murder takes place at all, such as the myth of Noah, for example" by stating:

> True, but in that myth there is a single survivor of an entire community doomed to death. In other words we are still dealing with an all-against-one structure, in this example, but reversed, and the reversal makes sense in terms of the mimetic theory in one of its most commonly inverted forms. The sacralized victim represents less of a loss of life than a return to life and the founding of a new community, which is clearly the case in the myth of the flood. The victim is the principle of survival. (Girard, 1987, p.39)

And later he adds that the all-against-one motif is, like any motif,

> susceptible to inversion, displacement, countless metamorphoses, and even, in some myths, complete disappearance. As we have seen there are some myths in which the victim is the sole survivor who, after having caused the downfall of an entire community, brings the latter back into being in a selective and differentiated manner. (p.114)

This is exactly the case with Zanarkand citizens, all killed so that they may become the fayth sustaining Sin, which certainly accounts for "a selective and differentiated manner". The "founding of a new community" of the earlier passage may be seen as both the evocation of the phantasmatic community of "Dream Zanarkand" and the constitution of the new community of Spira ruled by the Yevon cult. In its own special way, Yu Yevon's sacrifice of the whole of Zanarkand can be seen as his way to limit damages, since Zanarkand would have been destroyed anyway, and he could at least, so to speak, save face.

However, of course, the tightest connections between Spira and Girard consist in the Yevon cult instituted by Yunalesca and their way of handling Sin through the periodical repetition of the immolation of an innocent summoner, appeasing the monster for a while but not vanquishing it altogether. This is as close an image of the scapegoating described by Girard as we may ever get. The prohibition to use machines enforced by the clergy makes perfect sense in the logic of avoiding the original mimetic competition engendering Sin, and it is also consistent that the high clergy instead uses machines, since they know how to use them without risks. At the same time, the rituals prescribed by the clergy, however ineffective in defeating Sin once and for all, are effective in maintaining the Farplane, the world of the dead, separated from the lands of the living, and in keeping Sin at bay the most they believe they can. Most importantly, as rituals always are, both the Sending and summonings consist, even in variations, in endless repetitions of the same gestures, that is, in repeated imitations. The whole system is founded in Girardian anthropology. Even the presumed hypocrisy of the Yevonite priests in not telling the whole truth to the people is paralleled by the silence of the ancient pagan priests who could not expose the truth about the sacrificial procedure to the uninitiated because that would cause upheavals in the community.

Nonetheless, this is not the whole picture. On the contrary, what has insofar been said is just the stage upon which the actual play takes place, a play consisting precisely in the open denunciation, or rather, revelation, of the sacrificial dynamics to the whole wide world. In our reality, this revelation begins with Judaism, as the Old Testament already makes it clear that the designation of the victim is arbitrary, for many victims in the stories are innocent: Abel, Isaac, Joseph, Daniel... Furthermore, the very expression *scapegoat* comes from Jewish Law, prescribing the immolation of a goat to exorcise the sins of the community. It is a first step toward a more civil society, banning any killing. But that cannot take place before Jesus Christ, the Man who was God, in Girard's account, not because he was resurrected from the dead, but because he was the first who brought the sacrificial horror of scapegoating in broad sunlight, so that everybody may see and condemn it. This event, the greatest event in human history, is the only worthy of being called divine, for it redefined all civilization forever. In Spira, this is what happens first in the premonition of Auron, unwilling to sacrifice himself in his first pilgrimage with Braska and Jecht, but mostly the revelation of the vanity and arbitrarity of sacrifice does not come in refusing it, but in fully embracing it to save others, especially to save Yuna, as Tidus does, exposing to everybody the whole truth about Sin and Yevon. In this sense, it is possible to identify the deep Christian subtext of *FFX*, in a reading that is perhaps even more convincing after the release of *Final Fantasy XV*, whose protagonist Noctis is explicitly called the King of Kings.

Concerning the love story between Tidus and Yuna, he declares to her only after rescuing her from combined marriage with High Priest Seymour before they may exchange vows at their wedding ceremony, and Yuna reciprocates Tidus undoubtedly because of his self-confidence born from his admirers in Dream Zanarkand as a blitzball star. Theirs is a perfect combination of mimetic desires, and the outcome is tragic because Tidus's mimetic rivalry with Seymour may be resolved by sending Seymour's soul to the Farplane, but Yuna's mimetic rivalry with the whole Dream Zanarkand. requires the end of Dream Zanarkand for Yuna to win, but this entails also Tidus's end. In the parallelism already traced, the true marriage between Christ and the Church may only be fully accomplished in Heaven.

So, even as the final quote from *Ezekiel* in *Things Hidden Since the Foundation of the World* hinted at a possible belief by Girard in the actual resurrection of the dead and the afterlife, in Spira, at the end of the game, we are left with a world where organized religion was subverted, its god dead and proven to be false, and no other gods appear, but it is still a world where magic works and the afterlife is real. What should we make of it all? If we read the whole happening under the lens of Girardian theory, as I endeavoured to do, we may conclude that the old, secretive sacrificial system of scapegoating is the dead Yevon religion, and that subverting it was a divine act of Christ as represented by Tidus. This way, however painful the latter's disappearance, at this point feasible to be paralleling the Ascension, still his Spirit will guide his companions/disciples and Yuna/Mary, who in fact says that those who are gone will never be forgotten, in building the new, free society of Spira, that in historical reality would be the whole Christian world. If there is someone that can be taken seriously in looking at the whole history of mankind, especially as read by Girard, and saying, like Tidus does: "This is my story", there is no doubt that he would be the Man-God, Jesus Christ, and his, like the 2001 commercial for *FFX* said, would be a story of purity and love.

Bibligraphy

Caldwell, K.E.H., 2013. *Digital "Fayth" and Ritual "Play": A Study in Religious Participation and Audiovisual Affect in Contemporary Video Games*. Senior Honors Thesis: University of Wisconsin-Madison.

---, 2015. Acting in the Light and on Fayth: Ritualized Play. *Journey and Final Fantasy X. Well Played*, 4(1), pp.157-178.

Daliot-Bul, Michal, 2009. ASOBI IN ACTION. *Cultural Studies*, 23(3), pp.355-380.

Eisner, A.J., 2017. *Student Independent Projects Historical Studies 2017: Human Freedom: Existential Philosophy in Video Games*. Research Report. Grenfell Campus, Memorial University of Newfoundland (Unpublished). Available at: <https://research.library.mun.ca/13142/> [Accessed 28/06/2022].

Girard, R., 1987. *Things Hidden Since the Foundation of the World*. Stanford: Stanford University Press.

Greenfield-Casas, S.X., 2017. *Between Worlds: Musical Allegory in Final Fantasy X*. MM Thesis: The University of Texas at Austin.

Hahn, D., 2009. Sin, Otherworldliness, and the Downside to Hope. In: J.P. Blahuta and M.S. Beaulieu, eds. 2009. *Final Fantasy and Philosophy: The Ultimate Walkthrough*. Hoboken, NJ: John Wiley & Sons. pp.151-165.

Huber, W., 2007. Fictive affinities in *Final Fantasy XI*: complicit and critical play in fantastic nations. In: S. De Castell, and J. Jenson, eds. 2007. *Worlds in Play: International Perspectives on Digital Games Research*. New York: Peter Lang Publishing. pp.169-178.

Likarish, P., 2014. Filtering Cultural Feedback: Religion, Censorship, and Localization in *Actraiser* and Other Mainstream Video Games. In: H.A. Campbell and G.P. Grieve, eds. 2014. *Playing with Religion in Digital Games*. Bloomington & Indianapolis: Indiana University Press. pp.170-190.

Luft, S., 2014. Hardcore Christian Gamers: How Religion Shapes Evangelical Play. In: H.A. Campbell and G.P. Grieve, eds. 2014. *Playing with Religion in Digital Games*. Bloomington & Indianapolis: Indiana University Press. pp.154-169.

Menard, M.K., 2008. *The Creation of Emotion in Games: A look at the Development of Player Emotional Responses in a Global Environment Using the Six 'Primal' Emotions*. MA Thesis: Savannah College of Art and Design.

Schut, K., 2013. *Of Games and God: A Christian Exploration of Video Games*. Grand Rapids, Michigan: Brazos Press.

Sjølie, K.F., 2018. *Procedural Religion in Videogames. A narratological and ludological analysis of how religious ideas are reflected, rejected and reconfigured in Final Fantasy X and Bloodborne*. MA Thesis: University of Oslo.

Washburn, D., 2009. Imagined History, Fading Memory: Mastering Narrative in *Final Fantasy X*. Mechademia, Vol. 4, pp.149-162.

Heaven, Hell, and Virtual Reality

Mark Kirkbride

Abstract

Virtual reality (VR) is the ultimate example of Baudrillard's hyperreality. In fiction, it can be mapped onto first world, fantasy or religious templates. Science fiction (SF) has outlined many ways to defy death that dispense with religion, yet in usurping the place of religion at the point of death, VR bears distinct parallels with it. Here, rather than attempting to supersede religion, science fiction makes conscious use of religious and specifically Christian conceptions of immortality to demarcate the boundaries between life and a VR afterlife together with the manner of migration between them. As exemplified in novels such as Greg Egan's *Diaspora* (1997), Peter Watts' *Blindsight* (2006), Iain M. Banks' *Surface Detail* (2010) and Neal Stephenson's *Fall; or, Dodge in Hell* (2019), and in series such as *Upload* (2020, 2022), SF falls back again and again on religious analogies: between upload and ascension, backups and resurrection, storage and Limbo, and download and the Second Coming. Sometimes the mapping of the virtual afterlife onto a religious template is implicit, sometimes—as in *Surface Detail* and *Upload*—explicit. Science fiction then complicates these religious foundations as each work featuring VR resets the parameters. Yet the moral dimension is often retained as free will means that suffering and—given imperfect Heavens, perfect Hells—even *physical* pain carries over into virtuality along with the concept of sin. Christian transhumanists have claimed that virtual reality will provide the means for an actual digital resurrection. Here, far from competing, science and religion converge. Both in science fiction and postulated fact, religion provides a lexicon and a blueprint for a virtual afterlife.

Introduction

The one based on faith and the other on fact, religion and science inevitably differ on death, with religious and virtual reality afterlives in SF an exception. Wagner notes of religion and virtual reality (interpreting the latter widely) that both 'can be viewed as manifestations of the desire for transcendence' (Wagner, 2012, p.4). Science fiction has found many ways to envisage life after death (Burt, 2014), not least the transfer of consciousness from a failing body into a new one in a continuation of life as in *Altered Carbon* (2002). Absolute death is avoided, corporeality is maintained and any testing of the validity of a religious afterlife is postponed. If, however, the transition is from one plane (mortal) to another (immortal) in a closed environment where consciousnesses can interact with other consciousnesses likewise freed from temporal bonds, comparisons with religious and especially Christian conceptions of an afterlife immediately come into play. Plenty of works have explored virtual reality, from the glimmerings of VR in *Neuromancer* (1984) to a recognisable alternative reality in *Snow Crash* (1993) and beyond. I refer, however, to full immersion—living, post-death, inside virtual reality, with VR providing the means of immortality—as envisioned in novels such as *Surface Detail* (2010) and TV series such as *Upload* (2020, 2022).

The Mapping of the Virtual Environment onto First World, Fantasy and Religious Templates

As a life-sized three-dimensional map, virtual reality is the ultimate example of Baudrillard's hyperreality. In a virtual reality afterlife, VR is the only reality, for "Never again will the real have the chance to produce itself—such is the vital function of the model in a system of death, or rather of anticipated resurrection, that no longer even gives the event of death a chance" (Baudrillard, 1994, p.2). Writers of VR worlds can choose between a recognisable reality, a removed first world as in the Egdod era of Bitworld in Neal Stephenson's *Fall; or, Dodge in Hell* (2019) (hereafter, *Fall*), and a made-up world, as in the El vision of Bitworld that incorporates elements of (medieval) fantasy. Much of *Fall* details the tussle between these two competing visions of eternity. Yet in addition to first world and fantasy, a third option is available: the religious template. This goes beyond the creation and burgeoning of new worlds in early Bitworld or in Greg Egan's *Diaspora* (1997) that invite comparisons with the Book of Genesis or even naming virtual environments, as in Peter Watts' *Blindsight*, "Heaven" (Watts, 2006, p.37).

Upload/Ascension

Christian and virtual afterlives possess a number of features in common, including, as mentioned, the shift from a mortal to an immortal state, the concomitant shedding of corporeality and the arrival in a closed community. The distinct religious connotations of the transition itself, from an earthly plane to another plane altogether, do not escape notice or comment in VR texts. In *Blindsight*, the uploaded are referred to as "the Ascended" (Watts, 2006, p.143). Technically, Siri Keeton's mother Helen is not dead – though it is implied that there is no going back. Her body is in suspended animation pending "that final technological breakthrough that would herald the arrival of the Great Digital Upload" (Watts, 2006, p.37). When Siri visits his mother in her customised heaven, his "new inlays […] shook hands with the noosphere and knocked upon the Pearly Gates" (Watts, 2006, p.143). If expressed in colloquial terms, the parallel between upload and ascension could not be made clearer.

Relationship to the Real

Despite the obvious one-to-one correspondences between heaven and VR, manifold differences obviously exist. For example, families can visit and communicate directly with their loved ones in *Blindsight*, and likewise in *Upload*. In *Fall*, separation is complete and communication is impossible but those left behind can still observe those on the other side. Extra complexities are explored such as different operating speeds between VR and what Iain M. Banks terms "the Real" (Banks, 2010, p.46), which is the case in *Surface Detail* in passing, and *Diaspora* and *Fall* in depth, as each work of science fiction resets the parameters.

Death/Deletion and Digital Resurrection

If virtual reality removes the fear of death, it is replaced by the fear of deletion. This possibility is presented as a secret in *Surface Detail*, where some of those who are missing and presumed to be in Hell have simply been deleted. Yet deletion is not always catastrophic. Just as the Bible suggests that the dead will be brought back for the Last Judgement, so the VR dead can be regenerated from previous backups. The "neural lace" technology in *Surface Detail*, which records one's experience over time, can result in a "a perfect copy" of consciousness (Banks, 2010, p.78). This is how Lededje

Y'breq survives her own murder. With digital resurrections, recent memories are lost but not everything is. Sometimes multiple copies of the same individual with completely different life experiences can exist simultaneously, as in *Diaspora*. For those tired of immortality, VR worldbuilders leave open the option of "a second, final, absolute death" (Banks, 2010, p.128), namely, reabsorption into the virtual environment—information to information, pixels to pixels.

Storage/Limbo

In the analogy between a Christian afterlife and a virtual one, the Limbo of Catholic theology bears comparison with the state of those awaiting upload. Much of *Surface Detail* is about the Hells. Those missing from the Heavens or the Hells are "In limbo", "Stored, but not functioning, not in any living sense" (Banks, 2010, p.259). Limbo in VR is not a specific place, yet it is the absence of a designated destination.

Download/The Second Coming

It might be thought that the portability of consciousness between the virtual and the real in Egan's hard SF *Diaspora* precludes pronounced religious analogies, yet a religious component declares itself when Yatima and Inoshiro leave the safety of the polis and copy themselves into gleisner robots to try and encourage "fleshers" to escape impending apocalypse. Despite attempting to save mankind from suffering and pain, Yatima and Inoshiro meet suspicion and resistance. A "static" says of their "insipid virtual paradise", "We humans are fallen creatures; we'll never come crawling on our bellies into your ersatz Garden of Eden. […] there will always be flesh, there will always be sin" (Egan, 1997, p.110). The pair's joint Christlike mission is rebuffed and the non-believers perish. In *Upload*, Pastor Rob says "Download is worse blasphemy than upload. Only one download ever occurred. And it was Christ our Lord." Nora continues the identification of Nathan with the Saviour, only this time non-negatively, claiming that Nathan is willing to risk his life "to save the poor". She even challenges Pastor Rob, "[…] would you leave heaven to save the rest of us?" (*Upload*, 2022) Here the comparison made between the Second Coming and the downloading of consciousness is so explicit as to be on the nose.

The Moral Dimension: Free Will, Sin, Suffering and Pain

Although in VR, as in heaven, the absence of corporeality apparently means the end of physical pain, the psychological variety is still a factor. Bound up with free will, it remains a possibility even in the posthuman Konishi Polis of *Diaspora*, where, with intervention ruled out, the "inalienable right to madness and suffering" (Egan, 1997, p.15) is preserved. The choice, or rejection, of a virtual afterlife involves its own moral dilemmas. Early in *Upload*, it transpires that Nora's father "doesn't think heaven could be heaven without Mom in it" (*Upload*, 2020). Post-death, he can either maintain a relationship with his daughter from the virtual environment Lakeview or be reunited with his wife in a traditional afterlife. He cannot do both and the prospect that soothes him troubles his daughter. Yet if choices or chance mean that some suffering inevitably carries over into the virtual afterlife, surely there would be no need to *re-introduce* physical suffering, to *design in* pain, or to *reinstate* the concept of sin.

Virtual Heavens, Virtual Hells

While Neal Stephenson's 2019 novel *Fall* playfully compares VR to Hell in its title, whole portions of Banks' *Surface Detail* are set in a virtual Hell filled with torments as excruciating as they are convincing. The novel's Hells are populated by people and demons, with torture meted out as an object lesson to everyone else. Some, like Representative Errun, believe in the Hells. Others consider them barbaric and cruel, occasioning a backlash. The Hells provide much of the plot in the form of a war "amongst the Heavens, between the Afterlives" (Banks, 2010, p.117). Both sides fight in a simulation to determine the fate of the Hells. While those who die in battle are brought back to fight again, those who die in Hell come back to suffer further. Oblivion is preferable to Hell because it means an end to suffering (Banks, 2010, p.279). Chay Hifornsdaughter, an academic trying to bring an end to the Hells, experiences one first-hand. While "The Hell had been virtual, […] the experiences and the suffering had felt entirely real" (Banks, 2010, p.345). Hence it is appropriate that her subsequent incarnation is as an angel of death which, in Hell, is an angel of mercy. VR afterlives include not only imperfect Heavens, but also perfect Hells.

Faith in the Future and a Retrospective Heaven

Speculation about a merging of technology and consciousness, of science and religion, is not confined to fiction. At present, a religious afterlife and a virtual afterlife both require faith. Yet for some, the two are not at odds. Instead, they converge at a point in the future when virtual reality provides the means by which heaven will be realised. Tipler (1995) put forward the suggestion (in the Omega Point Theory) that the energy released by a collapsing universe would enable a supercomputer to resurrect the dead in VR. As Michael Shermer observes, "Since this far future supercomputer is, for all intents and purposes, omniscient and omnipotent, it is God" (Shermer, 2018, p.140). Eric Charles Steinhart postulates, via the Simulation Hypothesis, that we are already in a simulation and that its Engineers will promote us to a superior simulation, with promotion as resurrection and salvation. Such theories rely on a series of nested assumptions, all of which need to be correct. Shermer's debunking of them (Shermer, 2018, pp.140-41) demonstrates that they are more wishful thinking than science, but they represent perhaps the ultimate linking—the attempted unification—of science and religion. As Banks notes in *Surface Detail*, "once it was possible to copy a creature's mind-state you could […] start to make at least part of your religion real" (Banks, 2010, p.120). This is faith in computing power as faith in God.

Conclusion

SF solves the problem of death and it might be thought that science would therefore replace religion within it. In VR fiction, however, science replaces religion so thoroughly that the technological afterlife ends up resembling its religious counterpart. SF writers make repeated use of religious and specifically Christian analogies between mortality and immortality and the manner of passage between them: between upload and ascension, backups and resurrection, storage and Limbo, and download and the Second Coming. Sometimes the points of comparison are implicit. In works such as *Surface Detail* and *Upload*, they are explicit. SF plots complicate these religious foundations. Yet trends in science and technology in this area have been extrapolated into the future outside fiction too, with Christian transhumanists contending that computing power will increase to such an extent that VR will be able to recreate the world in a digital resurrection for all. After centuries offering alternative explanations, this would perhaps represent the final rapprochement between religion and science, with the one charting the unknown for the other.

Bibliography

Banks, I. M., 2010. *Surface Detail*. London: Orbit.

Baudrillard, J., 1994. *Simulacra and Simulation*. Translated from the French by Sheila Faria Glaser. Ann Arbor: The University of Michigan Press.

Burt, S., 2014. Science Fiction and Life after Death. *American Literary History*, 26(1), pp.168-90. <https://doi.org/10.1093/alh/ajt063>.

Download, 2022. Upload, series 2 episode 7. Available through: Amazon Prime Video [Accessed 21 August 2022].

Egan, G., 2008. *Diaspora*. London: Victor Gollancz Ltd.

Five Stars, 2020. Upload, series 1 episode 2. Available through: Amazon Prime Video [Accessed 20 August 2022].

Shermer, M., 2018. *Heavens on Earth: The Scientific Search for the Afterlife, Immortality and Utopia*. London: Robinson.

Steinhart, E.C., 2014. *Your Digital Afterlives: Computational Theories of Life After Death*. Basingstoke: Palgrave Macmillan.

Stephenson, N., 2019. *Fall; or, Dodge in Hell*. London: HarperCollins.

Wagner, R., 2012. *Godwired: Religion, Ritual and Virtual Reality*. Oxon: Routledge.

Watts, P., 2006. *Blindsight*. New York: Tor Essentials.

Background Reading/Viewing

Gibson, W., 1984. *Neuromancer*. London: Victor Gollancz Ltd.

Morgan, R., 2002. *Altered Carbon*. London: Victor Gollancz Ltd.

Stephenson, N., 1993. *Snow Crash*. London: Penguin Books.

Segal, A. F., 2004. *Life After Death: A History of the Afterlife in the Religions of the West*. London: Doubleday.

Tipler F. J., 1995. *The Physics of Immortality: Modern Cosmology, God and the Resurrection of the Dead*. London and Basingstoke: Macmillan.

Upload, 2020. [series 1] Available through: Amazon Prime Video [Accessed 20 August 2022]

Upload, 2022. [series 2] Available through: Amazon Prime Video [Accessed 21 August 2022]

The Sacred and Profane- UFO Religions and Alien Messiahs in *Rendezvous with Rama*

Kevin Cooney

Abstract

When Arthur C. Clarke crafted *Rendezvous with Rama* (1973), it came on the heels of the epic and wildly popular *2001: A Space Odyssey* (1968). Over the decades, Clarke stretched readers' imaginations with sweeping and awe-inspiring stories that tapped into the basic human instinct of curiosity. What Clarke rarely dabbled in was the subject of religion. While he touched on the subject in short stories and briefly in later novels, it was in *Rendezvous with Rama* that Clarke created a religion based on UFOlogy and ideas of an alien Messiah. For all of *Rendezvous with Rama*'s hard science and fetishistic technological detail, the heart and hero of the tale is the novel's only religious devotee. Acting as a servant of scientific truth and an alien God, Clarke's character of Boris Rodrigo is an exemplary link between the sacred and the profane in the history of science fiction.

*

Based on his decades of work, the science fiction luminary Arthur C. Clarke would never be confused for a religious apologist or crypto-theist. The hundreds of short stories and novels replete with soaring speculations on the technological potency of alien races and the latent promise of humanity left little room for ruminations on, or devotions to, gods. Yet, buried within Clarke's corpus, is a strain of awe and wonder not dissimilar to a religious experience. In *Rendezvous with Rama*, Clarke cut from holy cloth the Fifth Church of Jesus-Cosmonaut, a tantalizing faith that posits Jesus Christ was an extraterrestrial and his Earthly acolytes a sophisticated space-faring sect. The Fifth Church of Jesus-Cosmonaut possesses a weight beyond its light strokes because Clarke draws on the popular history of UFO lore and the seemingly contradictory nature of scientists with devout faith. In *Rendezvous with Rama*, Clarke reveals a religion whose God is an alien, and his astronaut followers are critical to the moment of crisis because to act in the service of science and humanity is to serve God.

Rendezvous with Rama was released five years after Clarke's seminal novel *2001: A Space Odyssey* (1968). The novel begins with a meteorite devastating Italian cities in 2077, leading to Earth's nations' creation of Spaceguard, a surveillance and defense system against planet-harming meteors. Fifty years after the creation of Spaceguard, a strangely behaving meteor appears on the radar screen of the solar system's defense network. Just beyond Jupiter, marked by an astounding size and following an atypical path, a meteor, dubbed Rama after the Hindu deity, was first seen. A probe sent to analyze the speedy and rolling object revealed no rocky features but a fifty-kilometer-long perfect cylinder. Dispatched to survey and possibly examine the Rama is the science vessel Endeavor and its crew, including communications officer Boris Rodrigo. As the Endeavor's crew unlocks the massive vessel, with Clarke delivering dizzying descriptions of a spinning O'Neill-style cylinder, Rama is revealed as a dead world pushing through the solar system. Over time, the Endeavor crew realizes Rama is not extinct but dormant, a mobile world set up to support life in odd cities, next to churning seas and beneath cloudy skies. While *Rendezvous with Rama* is told mainly through the perspective of the ship's commander, Norton, it is Rodrigo's religiosity that plays a vital part in determining the outcome of the hurtling Rama. The alien generation ship becomes an object of fear for Earth and its sister planets colonized over the centuries. Rama's strange movements lead some to conclude it is a weapon and should be stopped by another human-crafted weapon. With the support of his decidedly atheistic commander, Rodrigo is ready to intercept the human-designed weapon, suggesting a religious comfort with possible death. Through the lens of the Fifth Church of Jesus-Cosmonaut, Rodrigo sees the enigmatic Rama better than any other astronaut; Rama is an object of scientific revelation and/or religious salvation. Only through the unique blend of science and religion, knowledge and faith, does Clarke's "Cosmo Christer" become the key member of the Endeavor crew at the novel's climactic moment.

Religion and Arthur C. Clarke may not leap to the fore in analyzing science fiction and religion. A survey of Clarke's works finds fleeting engagements with religion, despite the author's decidedly atheistic credibility. The best examples of Clarke's literary visit with religion come in *The Star* (2000) and *The Nine Billion Names of God* (2000). In *The Star*, a Jesuit astrophysicist travels to a star that shone over Bethlehem. While in *Nine Billion Names of God*, Tibetan monks seek the aid of a computer system to calculate all the possible names of the divine, and as it finishes, the stars in the night sky above the Himalayan monastery begin to wink into darkness. Gary Westfahl notes Clarke is obliged "to sometimes acknowledge that religions can have beneficial effects" (2018, p.135). As a result, Westfahl writes, the science fiction author "describes the sporadic persistence of old religions, or emergence of new religions" (2018, p.135). In a 1968 *Playboy Magazine* interview, *2001: A Space Odyssey*, Clarke collaborator director Stanley Kubrick said, "the God concept is at the heart of 2001—but not any traditional, anthropomorphic image of God" (1968, p.94). Instead, Kubrick asserts extraterrestrials would become a disembodied intelligence that "would possess the twin attributes of all deities—omniscience and omnipotence" that could only be conceived as gods should "the tendrils of their consciousness ever brushed men's minds, it is only the hand of God we could grasp as an explanation" (1968, p.94). Decades later, this concept found its way into 1997's *3001: The Final Odyssey*, Clarke's final novel of the Monolith series. Westfahl observes that Clarke "endorses the notion that advanced aliens are equivalent to the gods of ancient religions" and "man's investigation of the monoliths is related to his' quest for God' (2018, p.142). In the future, as Clarke saw it, religion lingered and left fingerprints on society and in the daily activities of a few humans. One of Clarke's literary personages, born of Earth, followed a faith more grounded in reality than many could imagine.

Faith

> (Rodrigo was) a devout member of the Fifth Church of Christ-Cosmonaut. Norton … was equally in the dark about the church's rituals and ceremonies. But the main tenant of its faith was well known. Its members believed that Jesus Christ was a visitor from space, and an entire theology had been constructed on that assumption. (Clarke, 1973, p.69)

Even as hazily but enigmatically sketched as the Fifth Church of Jesus-Cosmonaut is, it is a faith with theological intrigue and historical precedent. Jesus Christ, son of God, the product of the Immaculate Conception and savior of humanity, was not a child of Nazareth but the cosmos. Christ was an extraterrestrial may sound like a skeptical writer's jab at organized religion and its followers. Clarke, however, knew the minutiae of the UFO lore as he described himself once in an episode of the television series *Arthur C. Clarke's Mysterious World* as a "reluctant expert" on the subject (LowFlyingAircraft, 2022). So deeply immersed in UFOlogy as he was, Clarke would undoubtedly know of would-be UFO prophets and seers who proclaimed Christ was an extraterrestrial. Clarke delicately traced the outlines of a classic syncretic religion, a faith blending mystery and magic with fetishization and adoration of technology.

Soaked into Clarke's "Cosmo Christers" are many attributes found in real-world UFO faiths like the Aetherius Society, followers of the Uranian Book, and George Van Tassel's Ashtar Command. Most importantly, these groups positioned Jesus Christ, and by extension the Christian Bible, at the center of their exo-theology. Ideas of placing Christ in the distinctly technologically focused world of UFOs were observed by Douglas Curran in his survey of UFO communities across North America. The spiritual message of the alien visitors was firmly rooted in Judeo-Christian tradition," emphasizing that "Every single flying-saucer group I encountered in my travels incorporated Jesus Christ into the hierarchy of its belief system" (Curran, 1985, p.23). Christ was no mere attractor for UFO devotees of the 20th century; the prophet was vital to delivering a message of salvation via flying saucers and their extraterrestrial occupants. The Fifth Church of Jesus-Cosmonaut comes into focus when lensed through the leading terrestrial faiths of the last century.

In 1954, British citizen George King was allegedly contacted by an extraterrestrial intelligence via telepathy. The alien "Master Aetherius" declared King to be the head of a movement to save the planet Earth. Aetherius revealed that Jesus Christ was born on Venus and sent to Earth as a helper to humanity. The intertwined, if not outright knotted, theology of the Aetherius Society was captured as, "Earth is a classroom on the evolutionary ladder of life" and "Jesus, Buddha, Krishna and other religious leaders were of extraterrestrial origin and came to Earth to help mankind" (Saliba, 2003, p.128). Sharing this cosmic seeding idea was George Van Tassel's Ashtar Command, founded on the belief that the Bible contained facts that were misinterpreted by the scientifically naive of the time. As Christopher Helland wrote of Ashtar Command's belief system, "Jesus was viewed as a more evolved being that came to Earth to assist in delivering humankind from the planet" and "did not die, rather was 'taken up on the transistor beam' after he had established the foundation for his cosmic return," via a fleet of spaceships (2004, p.167).

An echo of this idea can be heard in *Rendezvous with Rama* after Rodrigo reveals a fragment of the faith. When questioned by mission commander Norton about his religious take on the discovery of Rama, Rodrigo replies, "Our faith has told us to expect such a visitation, though we do not know exactly what form it will take. The Bible gives hints," saying shortly after, "I believe that Rama is a cosmic Ark, sent here to save" (Clarke, 1973, pp.121). While addressing Norton, an avowed but respectful skeptic, Rodrigo hints at the complex theology of an alien Christianity. Whereas Rama is of secular importance to Earth and Rodrigo, only the communications expert reads the alien vessel as Biblical hermeneutics. To Rodrigo, Rama is like Noah's Ark, a vessel that possesses the promise of salvation and revelations. In Rama, Rodrigo has a scientist's dream—a massive sprawling alien ship full of remarkable technology that would take decades to unravel. At the same time, Rodrigo must have experienced religious exultation at the prospect of unverified beliefs made real. However, from what and when, the astronaut is forced to ask. What form Rodrigo's Christianity takes is left to the reader's imagination. But in *Rendezvous with Rama*, Clarke suggests a strangeness in the faith, "Norton could never understand how men with advanced scientific and technical training could possibly believe some of the things he had heard Cosmo Christers state as incontrovertible fact" (1973, p.69). Following the UFO religion roadmap, there is a compelling analog in the form of the Urantia Book. This enigmatic volume claims to be a complete retelling of the Christian Bible from an extraterrestrial perspective. In her essay, The Urantia Book, Sarah Lewis writes, "aims to unite science, religion and philosophy, noting that, when viewed separately, these three disciplines are unable to answer the fundamental question of existence" (2003, p.129). Lewis explains that the Urantia Book, the extraterrestrial name for Earth, is a collection of five "revelations" with the retelling of the rebellion in Heaven, but as an extraterrestrial tale, the story of Adam and Eve, a variation of the story of Biblical king-priest Melchizedek, and the life of Jesus (2003, p.130). For the latter revelation, Christ becomes a "Creator Son," creator and ruler of the Urantia's celestial region, our universe (2003, p.131).

Underlying these UFO faiths is a system of interpretive theology and anxieties around 20th-century technological advances. Each new religion sought to blend ancient traditions, leveraging their cache and reassuring emotional facets while answering Earthly technological leaps by suggesting greater alien intelligence who sought to care for humanity during the turbulent decades after World War II. Rather than calling the UFO religions "scientific religions," Christopher Partridge suggests the framing of "physicalist religion" (2003, p.22) because such faiths combined New Age ideas with "pseudo-technological interpretations of traditional religious beliefs" (2003, pp.22-23). Though Clarke's Fifth Church of Jesus-Cosmonaut could follow those traditions and wear the label of "physicalist religion", *Rendezvous with Rama* asserts the fictional faith as a harmonizing balance between faith and reason. Rodrigo's actions upon discovering the Rama, through his own surveys of the ship and ultimate heroic act, show a finely if impossibly well-tuned personality and morality. Albert Einstein could have also been describing the Fifth Church follower when he admitted he could not "conceive of a genuine scientist without that profound faith. The situation may be expressed by an image: science without religion is lame, religion without science is blind" (1960, p.46). Never once abandoning scientific principles, Rodrigo's faith in an alien Jesus only comes into play when the Rama vessel and the Endeavor crew is under threat. The astronaut makes a life-changing decision without hesitation as Rama is a test of his faith and his belief in the survival of hope. None of these concepts are explicitly explored by Clarke, but it is implied that as the story climaxes, Rodrigo's curiosity and faith come together. Because to act in the service of science and the faith is to walk in step with God.

Piety and Duty to the Stars

> It was perhaps not surprising that an unusually high proportion of the church's devotees worked in space in some capacity

or other. Invariably, they were efficient, conscientious, and absolutely reliable. (Clarke, 1973, p.69)

When asked if science and faith were antagonists, NASA's German-born lead rocket engineer Werner Von Braun said the contrary was true, "they are sisters. While science tries to learn more about the Creation, religion tries to better understand the Creator" (Noble, 1997, p.127). In *Rendezvous with Rama*, the secular space service is peopled with technicians and specialists of religious faith, those "Cosmo Christers" as the backbone of this scientific corps. Von Braun, whose previous Nazi affiliations were obscured in the years after World War II, expressed a Christian core to space exploration that surely played to the language of American Bible Belt taxpayers. The face of NASA during its heyday, Von Braun, believed "the life of Jesus Christ should be the focus of our efforts and inspiration" (Noble, 1997, p.128). Science in the service of God, while seemingly foreign to 21st-century minds, has a long and distinct history that Clarke embraces, even briefly, in *Rendezvous with Rama*.

A roster of history's most remarkable and boldest scientific and mathematic thinkers is also a list of believers in God—Nicolaus Copernicus, Sir Isaac Newton, Johannes Kepler, etc. Catholic Copernicus, in 1543's *De Revolutionibus Orbium Coelestium*, dedicated the tome to Pope Paul III and noted early in Chapter One that the natural philosopher's pursuits were only possible "by the grace of God, without whom we can accomplish nothing" (Copernicus, 1543). Copernicus never wavers in citing his faith in God and seeks permission, amid his confessed audacity, to argue his case for the sun as the center of the solar system. For Copernicus and the following generations of natural philosophers to contemplate the mechanics of the cosmos was not heresy but rather an attempt to understand the mechanics of the divine creator's work. These luminaries were shadows of God the scientist. In *Rendezvous with Rama*, Rodrigo follows these same patterns, reveling in scientific discovery while serving an unseen alien God.

Clarke challenges Rodrigo through Norton's internal monologues, asking himself, "How would a man with such religious beliefs react to the awesome reality of Rama? Suppose he encountered something that confounded his theology- or, for that matter, confirmed it?" (1973, p.69). Clarke's astronaut commander's confident atheism displays a skepticism, if not fear, of how a pious individual may react in a moment of religious crisis. What Clarke subtly does in the character of Rodrigo is craft a person who will not waver when science and facts meet theological speculations. Internal conflicts incited by external influences will not be stoked precisely because faith bulwarks the soul, and science defends the intellect. Clarke, via Norton, exposes a bias by implying that religious belief is inherently unreliable and cannot withstand emotional or intellectual challenges. However, in Rodrigo, Clarke creates a scientist with unshakable faith and technical competency born from mastery of science. Not a theologian or monk who works in the sciences. A model of the pious scientist differing from Cosmo Christers was the Jesuit Astrophysicist in 1955's *The Star*. The Vatican-appointed scientist discovers a world extinguished by a star gone supernova that shone down on Bethlehem the night of Jesus's birth. Seeing the remnants of an alien civilization intentionally destroyed by an indifferent God or indiscriminately wiped out by a mechanistic system, Clarke's holy man falters in his faith when he realizes a world was simply destroyed to herald the birth of Christ. As lightly built as the character of Boris Rodrigo was, Clarke captured, "a person who is religiously enlightened appears to me to be one who has, to the best of his ability, liberated himself from the fetters of his selfish desires" (Einstein, 1960, p.44). Exposure to or studying Rama's unfathomable alien bulk does not test or measure Rodrigo's faith. An assault on the alien creation and humanity, however, does put the follower of the Fifth Church of Jesus-Cosmonaut's faith into action.

Apotheosis

> As for Rodrigo himself, he seemed to regard the possibility of instant apotheosis with complete equanimity. (Clarke, 1973, p.241)

For all of Clarke's skirting of the theological, the writer chooses a religiously potent word to describe Rodrigo ahead of the climax. Selecting apotheosis—the elevation to divine status—Clarke did not pick martyr or hero when describing Rodrigo's plan to intercept the Mercury-launched missile. Either noun would suffice, as the plan and its execution could also be labeled self-destruction. Yet, when a strategy is born from the sole religiously minded member of the Endeavor, the religious implications emerge. If the cosmos is ruled by complex processes and propulsive forces measured and outlined by mathematics, then why would Rodrigo, seemingly bound by the immutable natural laws, willingly sacrifice himself? The answer comes from the perspective of Robert Crawford, who contends, "Only the human can choose the truly altruistic preservation of the other at the expense of the self" (2004, p.71). The idea of a cosmic Christ, as suggested in Aetherius and Urantian, is also shadowed by Crawford, who writes, "he has a cosmic dimension relating not only to humanity but to all things" (2004, p.46). It is Crawford who also argues for a new model of the divine. Rather than a king or anthropomorphic representation, Christ is a suffering scientist (2004, p.45). I see Rodrigo following in the same path, a scientist curious and questioning but willing to sacrifice himself in defense of "all things" as well as the cause of humanity.

If we view Rodrigo's heroics through Crawford's perspective that the scientist "is a symbol of one who battles with disease and evil and can involve himself in risk" (2004, p.107), we see a clear line of Rodrigo. For most of the novel, Rodrigo is an explorer, probing the cavernous interior of the Rama with crewmates. He is cautious and inquisitive. However, as Rama's fate is jeopardized, Rodrigo puts his life at risk to combat a potential evil hurled at science and humanity. Push into Crawford further and his theory on Christ, the scientist, evolves as a battler of natural and human-made evils. "In his battle against evil (Christ) goes all the way to the cross and endures the worst that it can do," Crawford then pivots to the scientist who "often to make agonizing decisions and emerges from (their) laboratory exhausted" (2004, p.107) or suffering later of diseases or maladies brought on by their work. And in Crawford's mind, "The cosmic scientist is engaged in warfare against every kind of evil" (2004, p.108), and this cleanly intersects with Rodrigo's view of the cosmos through the lens of his religion.

When the Mercury leadership launches a destructive probe at Rama, Norton wonders how the Mercury way of thinking fits Fifth Church theology. Rodrigo replies, "Only too well, Commander... It's the age-old conflict between the forces of good and the forces of evil. And there are times when men have to take sides in such a conflict" (Clarke, 1973, p.239). *Rendezvous with Rama*'s lone religious devotee steps forward to not only offer a solution to the crisis but volunteers to carry it out. Evil is not a label applied to the elements or processes of the natural or formal sciences. Evolution is not evil when it selects out a species. A natural event takes on specific moralistic tones when humans point to the event or action and label it as good or evil. The Hermian government sending a missile to an unprecedented astronomic discovery can be seen as good as it is a preemptive move against potential danger. From the perspective of the Endeavor crew, the action is purely evil. Rodrigo could contradict God's plan by defusing the missile, but if the Fifth Church has any basis in traditional terrestrial morals, then intercepting a destructive device is clearly an act of benevolence. However, it is not an act without individual cost. It could fail, leading to the destruction of Rama and Rodrigo, with a cascade of crises possibly to follow. Should Rodrigo defuse the missile but die in the process, it becomes a selfless act done with a calm head because of implied spiritual salvation and ascension. Clarke's use of apotheosis demands that the reader view Rodrigo's decision as one of moral ascendency to a higher state. No other crew offers their services based on their moral compass. The extraordinary events at Rama carry a weight beyond that of a scientist seeking to save an alien artifact.

A selfless act born from a moralistic impulse nurtured from a religious upbringing saves not only science's most important discovery but also, possibly, humanity. It's essential to return to the point where only Rodrigo finds the solution and volunteers. Clarke never writes about the feverish plans and schemes hatched on spacecraft, planets, or moons between the Rama and the Mercury government launchpad.

The Endeavor crew fails to conjure up a solution as well. The heroic character in Clarke's science-dense fictional tale is not a sentiment machine or atheist astronaut but an acolyte of alien Christ. To pursue the missile, which we are left to speculate is deemed not part of God's plan while the Rama is, is an emulation of Christian sacrifice and apotheosis. Rodrigo is willing to sacrifice himself to 'save' not just Rama but the promises it holds for humanity. In this act, Clarke's Rodrigo engages a form of Christlike behavior—giving up his own life to save the human race. Rodrigo is guided by twin pillars—knowledge of science and the belief in an alien Christ. The morality of the kind tapped by Rodrigo is not a product of evolution in *Rendezvous with Rama*.

Arthur C. Clarke's Boris Rodrigo asks radical questions about the universe, his faith, and fellow humans. Centuries of thinkers asked the radical questions of the universe, the why and how of creation. But in many of Clarke's books, the inquisitive thinkers are often alien intelligences probing humanity with their near-supernatural technologies. The Rama does not theologically threaten Rodrigo; rather, the massive spaceship only arouses religious potential while exciting his scientific curiosity. His actions at the climax invite the reader to evaluate their perceptions of what happens when an extraterrestrial event occurs and grinds against detached scientific thinking, reactionary human instincts, and a handful of religious faithful. Rodrigo questions Rama and its unknown creators while searching within himself and sifting through the doctrines of his faith. He seeks answers to questions and posits solutions to seemingly insurmountable tests. Acting as a servant of scientific truth and an alien God, Boris Rodrigo is an exemplary link between the sacred and the profane in the history of science fiction.

Bibliography

Clarke, A.C., 1973. *Rendezvous with Rama*. Boston: Mariner Books.
---, 2000. *The Collected Stories of Arthur C. Clarke*. New York: TOR.

Copernicus, N., 1543. *De Revolutionibus Orbium Coelestium*. [online] Available at: <https://www.geo.utexas.edu/courses/302d/Fall_2011/Full%20text%20-%20Nicholas%20Copernicus,%20_De%20Revolutionibus%20(On%20the%20Revolutions),_%20l.pdf> [Accessed 5 September 2022].

Crawford, R., 2004. *Is God A Scientist?* New York: Palgrave Macmillan.

Curran, D., 1985. *In Advance of the Landing: Folk Concepts of Outer Space*. New York: Abbeville Press.

Einstein, A., 1960. *Ideas and Opinions*. New York: Crown Publishers.

Helland, C, 2003. *From Extraterrestrials to Ultraterrestrials*. In: C. Partridge, ed. 2003. UFO Religions. London: Routledge.

Lewis. S., 2003. The URANTIA Book. In: C. Partridge, ed. 2003. *UFO Religions*. London: Routledge.

Low Flying Aircraft, 2022. *Arthur C. Clarke's Mysterious World - Ep. 10 - U.F.O.s* [video online] Available at: <https://youtu.be/qD8ls6ybLhg> [Accessed 10 September 2022].

Noble, D., 1997. *The Religion of Technology*. New York: Alfred A. Knopf.

Partridge, C. 2003. Understanding UFO Religions and Abduction Spiritualities. In: C. Partridge, ed. 2003. *UFO Religions*. London: Routledge.

Saliba, J., 2003. The Earth is a Dangerous Place. In: J. Lewis, ed. 2003. *Encyclopedic Sourcebook of UFO Religions*. Ch.6. Chicago: Playboy.

That Eric Alper, 2018. *Playboy Interview: Stanley Kubrick*. [online] Available at: <https://www.thatericalper.com/2018/10/07/read-stanley-kubricks-full-interview-in-playboy-magazine-from-1968-playboy/?doing_wp_cron=1661180327.9907081127166748046875> [Accessed August 2022].

Westfahl. G., 2018. *Arthur C. Clarke*. Champaign: University of Illinois Press.

Contributors

Eugen Bacon MA, MSc, PhD is an African Australian author of several novels, prose poetry and fiction collections. She's a 2022 World Fantasy Award finalist, and was announced in the honor list of the 2022 Otherwise Fellowships for 'doing exciting work in gender and speculative fiction'. Her short story release *Danged Black Thing* received a 2021 Otherwise Award honor as a 'sharp collection of Afro-Surrealist work'. Recent books: *Mage of Fools* (novel), *Chasing Whispers* (short stories) and *An Earnest Blackness* (essays). Eugen has two novels, a novella and three anthologies (ed) out in 2023, including *Serengotti*, a novel, and the US release of *Danged Black Thing*. Visit her website at eugenbacon.com and Twitter feed at @EugenBacon.

Steph P. Bianchini is an Italian academic based in the UK. Steph is an Associate Professor and a member of the Royal Historical Society and worked over the last ten years on projects in social sciences, international relations, and humanities. They blog about sciences, speculative fiction, and history at earthianhivemind.net and edit the ezine "Frozen Wavelets" (https://frozenwavelets.com/) of speculative flash fiction and poetry.
As a fiction writer, Steph is a member of SFWA and HWA, writing under the byline Russell Hemmell. Their short stories and poetry have appeared in 100+ publications, including *Aurealis*, *Cast of Wonders*, *Departure Mirror*, *Flame Tree Press*, *The Grievous Angel*, and others.

Kevin Cooney is an expert in human ecology and graduate of Harvard University, Kevin Cooney is an independent scholar, freelance writer, and ecocritic. His interest in environmental issues and associated subjects embedded in uncanny and estrangement stories of horror and science fiction propels his work and analysis.

His previous work, features in BSFA Award Winning *Worlds Apart: Worldbuilding in Fantasy and Science Fiction*.

An up to date collection of his work can be found at https://linktr.ee/kcooney

Giovanni Carmine Costabile (MPhil) Italian independent scholar, translator, writer, teacher. He presents at conferences in Italy and abroad and has published in several international academic journals and volumes dedicated to the Middle Ages, Medievalism, and Tolkien. He is the author of a monograph on Tolkien in Italian ("Oltre le Mura del Mondo", 2018), of a commentary in English on Tolkien's essay *On Fairy-stories* ("The Road to Fair Elfland", 2022), and conducted authorized research in the Tolkien Archive in Oxford. He translated more than ten volumes both from Italian into English and from English into Italian. He is the Editor of Phronesis Publishers's 'Silmarilli' series of Tolkien criticism, and a writer for the 'Fellowship & Fairydust' foundation and magazine from Maryland. For Phronesis he is also the author of the high fantasy trilogy "Cronache di Arlen".

Catherine A. Coundjeris holds an M.F.A. from Emerson College and a M.A. in Children's Literature from Simmons College. A former elementary school teacher, she has also taught writing at both Emerson College and Urban College in Boston. Catherine's poetry is published in literary magazines, including *The Dawntreader*, *Paper Dragons*, *Kaleidoscope*, *Jalmurra*, *Cholla Needles*, *Bewildering Stories*, *The Raven Review*, *Open Door Magazine*, *Stone Hill Journal*, *Honeyguide*, *Zephyr Review*, *Phare*, *Blue Bird Word*, *Life and Legends*, and *Jonah Magazine*. She also has stories published in Proem, Quail Bell, and KeepThings on Instagram. She has recently published an essay, "Éowyn as Light Bearer," in an anthology from Luna Press called *Not the Fellowship. Dragon's Welcome!*. Currently she is working on a fantasy epic. Catherine is passionate about adult literacy and ESL learning and volunteers with her local Literacy Council. An avid reader she enjoys listening to music, watching movies, gardening, and swimming.

Mark Kirkbride lives in Shepperton, England. He is an Hourly Paid Academic at Middlesex University, teaching the Working as a Writer module. He is also an Arts and Literature Tutor at Royal Holloway. He is currently doing a PhD at Brunel.
He is the author of *The Plot Against Heaven, Game Changers of the Apocalypse* and *Satan's Fan Club*, originally published by Omnium Gatherum and in the process of being republished by Crossroad Press. *Game Changers of the Apocalypse* was a semi-finalist in the Kindle Book Awards 2019. His short stories can be found in *Under the Bed, Sci Phi Journal, Disclaimer Magazine, Flash Fiction Magazine, So It Goes: The Literary Journal of the Kurt Vonnegut Memorial Library, Titanic Terastructures* and *The Last Horizon*. His poetry has appeared in the *Big Issue*, the *Morning Star*, the *Daily Mirror*, *Neon Literary Magazine*, the *London Reader*, *The Climate Matters Anthology 2020 (Culture Matters/Riptide Journal)*, *Sein und Werden* and Horror Writers Association chapbooks.

He was longlisted in the SaveAs Writers' International Writing Competition 2021 and the AUB International Poetry Prize 2021, and shortlisted in the AONB Landscape category of the Ginkgo Prize 2021.
Mark is a member of the British Fantasy Society, the British Science Fiction Association, the Horror Writers Association and Clockhouse London Writers. He has been published in the British Science Fiction Association's magazine *Focus* and in *Inspire – Exciting Ways of Teaching Creative Writing*, Goldsmiths, University of London (2020).

Cheryl Morgan is a writer, editor, publisher and critic. She owns Wizard's Tower Press and has written for a variety of outlets including *Locus*, *The SFWA Bulletin*, *SFX*, *Clarkesworld*, *Strange Horizons*, *Holdfast Magazine* and *SF Signal*. She is, to her knowledge, the first openly transgender person to have won a Hugo Award.
In addition to her science fiction interests she lectures widely on transgender history.

Ivano Sassanelli (Bari-Italy 1986) is Adjunct Professor of Canon Law at the Apulian Theological Faculty of Bari. He was awered Bachelor's Degree in Theology at the Apulian Theological Faculty of Bari (2010), Licence in Canon Law at the Pontifical University of Saint Thomas Aquinas of Rome (2013), Doctorate in Canon Law at the Pontificial Lateran University of Rome (2015), Master Degree in Law at the LUM University of Casamassima-Bari (2017) and now is Ph.D. student in Bioethics at the Pontifical Athenaeum Regina Apostolorum of Rome. He is Director of the academic and interdisciplinary series of fantastic studies and contemporary culture "*Eucatastrophe*" by Dots Edizioni of Bari and Co-director of the series "*Diritto canonico, comparazione* *giuridica e multiculturalità*" at the Cacucci Editor of Bari. In the Tolkien's context he studies the relationship between *ethics, religion, communication* and *fantastic literature* and is a member of the Scientific Committee of the International Exhibition "*The Tree of Tales*". He has published several scientific articles and essays that have appeared in academic series and journals and monographs, including: *Il Professore e il Poeta. Viaggio nel desiderio umano con Tolkien e Dante* (Dots, Bari 2023), *Tolkien e il vangelo di Gollum* (Cacucci, Bari 2020). He is also the Co-editor of the book: "*Vive in fondo alle cose la freschezza più cara.*" *Percorsi umani, letterari e filosofici nella Terra di Mezzo di Tolkien* (Aracne, Roma 2021).

Barbara Stevenson is a Scottish author living in Orkney. She is a retired veterinary surgeon and has an Honours degree in German. She has a fascination for folk tales and Gothic horror movies. The fairy tales of Oscar Wilde enchanted her from a young age. She lives in a cottage near the sea, is currently studying for a diploma in herbal healing and fosters kittens for a cat charity on the island, but she is adamant that she is not a witch.

Elyse Welles studied abroad at Oxford University specialising in Tolkien studies, and was chosen as Millersville University's Outstanding English Major in 2017, although this is her first piece of published Tolkien scholarship. Selected as a 'Best Poet of 2022' by Free Verse Revolution, she is a regular contributor of poetry and nonfiction articles for *The Wild Hunt News*, *Witch Way Magazine*, *Sunflower Journal*, *Metaphysical Times*, *Full Moon Magazine*, and has appeared in *Yellow Arrow Journal* and *Gypsophila Magazine*, among others. Her debut novel, *Witch on the Juniata River*, is forthcoming from Running Wild Press in 2024. She also cohosts the Magick Kitchen Podcast, and is the creator of Seeking Numina, a community-led shop featuring products and events from sacred places around the world. Elyse shares her time between Greece and Pennsylvania, traveling often to spiritual places — from natural wonders to ancient temples. Read her works at seekingnumina.com.

www.ingramcontent.com/pod-product-compliance
Lightning Source LLC
Chambersburg PA
CBHW050359120526
44590CB00015B/1746